IMMACULATE MISCONCEPTIONS

IMMACULATE MISCONCEPTIONS

A Self-Help Book
For Former Catholics

SHERRY BISHOP

Veranda Press

ISBN 0-9648756-0-8

Library of Congress Catalog Card Number
95-90868

Design by Stephen Herold
Cover art by Charles Schultz
Typography and production by Lasergraphics

Published by Veranda Press
P.O. Box 626
Carlsborg, Wa 98324
(360) 681-0700

Printed in the United States.

ACKNOWLEDGMENTS

I would like to express my great thanks to all of the former Catholics who completed the questionnaire and to those who offered their experiences and ideas during interviews.

Thank you to my clients, who offered suggestions and courageously worked with many of the exercises described in the book.

Many thanks for the special help and support given by Marty Buccieri, Jim Stapleton, Marjorie Lewe, Marjorie Lewe-Brady, and my mother, Mary Lou Zich.

I am particularly grateful to my husband Martin, whose editing skills and emotional support were instrumental in helping to bring this book to fruition.

CONTENTS

PREFACE

I was raised as a Catholic, and received 16 years of Catholic education. During my early years, I was educated by the Sisters of Mercy and the Sisters of St. Joseph. In high school I was educated by the Dominicans, and in college, by the Sisters of St. Francis. I received religious training at every stage of my education, in increasingly more complex formats. I had a lot of fun in the Church in high school; I wrote songs and sang at guitar Masses. I connected warmly with fellow Catholics, including clergy. Despite many positive experiences, however, a number of significant spiritual and moral questions remained unanswered throughout the years. In talking with clergy I looked for clarity. I received a variety of responses, none of which made much sense to me. I was also vaguely aware that many of the unpleasant experiences of my earlier Catholic days created feelings of resentment and fear, but I didn't know how to process these. Ultimately, I left the Church. There were simply too many contradictions and impasses. For years, I didn't give any of it much further thought, until a difficult period in my early 30's made me aware of the need to begin to develop a spiritual life of my own. Up until this point I would not have distinguished the concept of a Spiritual life from a Religious life; but in my own case I began to feel the need to do so. I discovered that this required me to look closely at what I had been taught in the past, and to work on letting go of what no longer worked for me—even though I had thought that I had already done so, simply by leaving the Church and outwardly rejecting its trappings! This process has proven to be much more complex than I had thought. My Catholic childhood encouraged absolute devotion to the Church. In developing my own thought system I encountered with surprise and dismay a lot of resistance from parts of myself which had been trained to think (or not to think…) in very different ways.

My aim is to share experiences and observations—both my own and those of others. My initial goal was to find out if my experiences matched those of other recovering Catholics, and to learn ways in which they were different. In doing this writing I had many emotions. I have let myself feel these different emotions as the work progressed. Some of them were uncomfortable, some of them were pleasant and energizing. I have continued to work with the feelings and the issues of my own past. I see life as a process of constantly letting go of what is no longer useful, and moving forward. With that in mind, I certainly don't see myself or any of us as having all the answers and I hope that you will feel free to take what you need and leave the rest.

In order to gather material for this book, I devised a questionnaire about the experience of growing up Catholic. This questionnaire covered a broad array of topics and invited respondents to share not only their memories, but also their thoughts and feelings, both past and present. Some of those who responded also communicated their willingness to be interviewed. Some remained in contact with me through the writing of the manuscript and contributed additional material later on. These recovering Catholics represented an amazing array of experiences and world views. Some people chose not to participate, either due to time limitations or because the subject matter was too painful for them. Those who felt they were able to participate did so with great openness and willingness, completing the lengthy questionnaire or interview generously. Material was also gathered from private therapy clients who have worked with some of the exercises discussed in the book. I am grateful to all of these people, because I feel that much of what they have shared will have a healing effect on some of the readers.

The book is organized into two separate sections. The first section, entitled 'Legacies', explores some of the religious, moral and social teachings of the Catholic Church, with particular emphasis on how these impacted the lives of Catholics raised in the '30's, '40's and '50's. The second section, 'Tools for Healing', focuses on practical methods of moving beyond the emotional, psychological and spiritual blockages experienced by many Catholics who were raised during this era. It is my hope that this book may play a useful part in your own journey.

SECTION I
LEGACIES

CHAPTER ONE

GROWING UP CATHOLIC

When I was in 5th grade I wrote a sexy story about the Beatles on pink paper my Dad used to bring home from the office. I brought the story to school and it began to make the rounds in my classroom. I was a "good girl" type at school, but in 5th grade my hormones were really starting to kick in, and I was also enjoying the notoriety I was getting from my story. Unfortunately, it was soon to come to an end. Mrs. Brady's all-seeing eye spotted the scrunched up wad of papers as they accidently fell to the floor. She asked the nearest student to bring them to her desk and quietly read them while the class did other work. Meanwhile, I sat in a state of sheer terror, horrified at what I knew was about to happen. Mrs. Brady couldn't deal with me right away because we were about to have a class awards ceremony. My anxiety level continued to rise as I shamefully stared at the awards themselves—plastic statues of the Virgin Mary—all of whom stared back at me reproachfully.

This kind of anxiety has arisen periodically throughout my life, and has often been present in the writing of this book. How can this kind of image from childhood carry such weight *long after we have intellectually rejected it as invalid?* Seeking to answer this question has been my main endeavor in this work.

So who is this book for? It is for those of us who suffered as children from the rigid and moralistic teachings of the Catholic Church. It is for those of us who suffered then and continue to suffer now, in a variety of ways, because we were each taught that suffering *itself* is a wonderful and noble thing. It is for those of us who dutifully learned that the Body is both the Temple of the Holy Spirit and the Seat of all Shame. It is for all of us who continue to be devilled by shame, often without knowing why.

This book is for John:

> "As a teenager, I was ashamed of my body. I was ashamed of my sexuality, and I was scared to death of girls. I didn't go out with girls until I was in my early 20's. I wasn't just hiding my nose. I built this elaborate intellectual system about why women were inferior to men and unworthy of my intention, and had arguments which eloquently put down all of my dating friends; how foolish they were, etc. Underneath, there was a lot of confusion and shame and doubt, all of it stemming from what I learned through the Church."

John is one of thousands of American Catholics who grew up stained with Original Catholic Sin. The details of his story are unique, but the underlying themes are strikingly common. Many of us have convinced ourselves that we have laid to rest the pernicious influence of our Catholic childhood, but how successful have we truly been?

John goes on:

> "I had a thought yesterday. I've always seen myself as a very intellectual person and I've always believed I create my

own life. I see what the reality is and create that with an act of my mind, and if there's been years of horseshit and pain, well, pshww! I'll cut that off. *I'm* going to be who I wish to be; and I recognize that's not true but I still retain an illusion of that sort, and in particular, with regard to Catholicism. At age 22 or 23, in less than one day's time, I really looked at Catholicism and decided I couldn't accept any of that, and from then on I gave it very little more thought. I was not a Catholic anymore. That was it. I was on this Ph.d. track. I just realized one day that I didn't want to be Catholic, that I didn't want to do anything with physics. I got the degree I'd been wanting but realized the normal life I'd been leading I didn't want either. I arranged my life from then on. I became a hermit. A magic time for me. It was an incredibly *freeing* time. I realized that all of these things had been imposed on me by parents, teachers, priests, nuns. I knew enough to say I don't want to do it. I didn't know what I *did want.* I wanted to be alone to figure it out.

"In a way, it was easy. I simply wasn't Catholic anymore. That being my way, I saw Catholicism as an amusing part of my past but nothing to do with me anymore. It has just occurred to me recently that of course that's not true, and *in my molecules* I've got *Catholic* molecules. (Laughs). It's in the DNA. I don't even know how that gets expressed!

"I had an interesting conversation once with an English professor 10 years ago. He wanted something from me and I became defensive. He jokingly remarked: '*I* don't have a Roman Catholic tragic view of the universe.' It was probably true. I was probably doing a Catholic number on him in becoming very dramatic. I heard someone say once about Christians (and I think this is particularly true of Catholics) that everything *matters.* There's some final truth that matters and it's a tragic view. That tragedy matters. That you could end up going to hell for all eternity. *That* matters. There's right and there's wrong and it would be *horrible* if I espoused the wrong."

This book is also for Mary, who adds:

"I have been taught so well that when I started having doubts, I didn't look elsewhere but stayed in the Church; I tried many different Catholic churches, all the while being angry, but hoping there would be some place that could meet my needs; but I wasn't even sure what those needs were, because everything I'd been taught had been kind of *ritualized* in a way that *became* my needs, not because I chose them but because I had been taught them and they had infiltrated many parts of my life."

This book is for Glen:

"I came from a moderately devout family without a lot of questioning. I don't remember a lot of what happened, but I *do* remember coming home and my parents saying things like 'If that's what they said in school, that's what's going to happen.' They had total faith in the Catholic system and if there was something wrong, it was with *me*."

I've come to think of this as a kind of Double Jeopardy: the unyielding authority of the Church, in combination with the authority of our parents, effectively squashed any attempt at independent thought. For many of us, this has influenced our ability as adults to trust and develop our creative thinking.

So this book is for Patty, too.

"I do have a hard time saying 'no', saying what I want, enjoying myself too much and/or for too long, being the center of attention, feeling okay about not being virginal. Actually, the more I think about it, the more I see it in my life. I practically draw a blank at times when someone asks me what I want. My usual response is 'Well, whatever *you* want', whether it's concerning the kind of pizza we're getting, or sex, or how my work station is set up."

Patty wasn't taught to value her own judgment, and neither was Glen:

"We had a religion class in high school where we were supposedly allowed to talk openly about fatherhood, the Catholic Church, family, and sex. If anybody said anything that wasn't following the 'party line', we'd hear about it. The priest who led it would always allow discussion, but then at the very end of the class he'd tell you what you should be believing. It crystallized what I'd felt since the second grade, that *questioning wasn't allowed*, in reality."

Those of us who managed as adults to assert our independence still had to suffer the consequences. Here is what one recovering Catholic said about the issue of marriage to non-Catholics:

"It was a big no-no. Consorting with the enemy. It meant you had to get married in the rectory in street clothes, (a big downer), and swear your kids over to the Church. My oldest friend's sister married a divorced non-Catholic and was ostracized—completely disowned. I myself am 'going to hell'. I married a non-Roman Catholic. My mother, for two years after our marriage (in a mission in California, but which my parents boycotted), would refer to my husband as 'the pagan' or 'the heathen'. My father refused to speak to us for several years and still isn't over it, 14 years and 4 kids later."

This book is also for Joan:

"In terms of raising my children, again, it's that old stuff that *Catholic* is the only right thing to be and my children are baptized Catholic but now that I've joined a Lutheran Church, they're going to make their 1st Communion in a Lutheran Church and I don't think that *counts* in the Catholic Church, and uh-oh, what does that make my children? Does that make them Lutheran? And that's not good enough! All of this stuff is going on in my head and I have to constantly talk to myself and say, that's not what it's all about. I have to work to convince myself I can get strength and support in any other Church. In the Catholic Church I don't feel like they have been open to changing as times change and meeting peoples' needs in a caring, sincere way."

This book is for Mary Alice:

"I'm unclear as to what parts of myself are clearly the influence of the Catholic Church. That in itself is uncomfortable, since we are supposed to know the answer. What things about me have their origin in my family rather than the Church? Bearing in mind that it is a Catholic family, can the two be separated? I suspect not."

How were we taught? What were we taught? Unlike most other Christian churches, Catholicism is a culture (in the same way that Judaism is a culture) in that it operates as a separate, closed unit. Despite recent moves towards Ecumenism, the Church throughout this century has considered itself to be the One, True, Holy and Apostolic Church. As a result, other religious traditions and spiritual practices remained virtually unknown to us, while the tenets and mores of the faith were strengthened and cemented from within. We were discouraged from having contact with non-Catholics and required to find answers through the Church only. This created a kind of constriction which kept us from growing. Sometimes, of course, individual members questioned this; but the Church was waiting with the answers, and our questions were further dispelled at the thought that millions of other people in the world adhered to the Faith. With so vast a following, how *could* it be wrong? So this book is for James:

"All of the books were very Catholic books, with a Catholic slant. There was a lot of indoctrination to my mind, and unless you were an extraordinary free mind and able to see beyond the 360 degrees around you, it was impossible to go beyond. It took me a long time to realize there were other thoughts to think, other experiences beyond the Catholic experience. I think non-Catholics just cannot appreciate the power, the pervasiveness of Catholicism. We were taught that all other religions were errors. The nuns weren't sure if they (the Protestants) would go to hell but they sure had a difficult row to hoe. They were damaged goods. No doubt about it."

This book is also for Hilary, who shares how the Church's teachings affected her sexuality:

"I was sexually very repressed and was told by my Catholic mother that sex was something I would be instructed about by my husband. I thought at age 14 that you could get pregnant from kissing. The Catholic attitude about sex is all about a primal fear of the power of women's bodies, and a fear of a loss of control on the part of the male hierarchy."

The 1960's idea of guilt-free sex was, I think, an illusion to many of us. It is simply not possible to grow up in a sexually repressed environment, with lots of negative messages regarding the body, and then go out and truly enjoy our sexuality, despite the fact that many of us now in our 30's and 40's tried hard to accomplish just that. We pretended we were relaxed and easygoing, that we had separated from our parents and our Catholic roots, but we nevertheless retained many of our repressive and puritanical core beliefs about sex that had been so successfully instilled in us during our childhood.

This book is for Ann:

> "I had a lot of sexual experiences in my 20's—I really let rip. I had stopped being Catholic and was so glad to be free of my parents' confining views about sex, which they very much associated with the Church. The problem was, I could never really feel free, even though I always felt warmth towards the person I was involved with. The Church was sitting at the end of the bed the whole time".

This book is for Bill and Trish and others who responded to the question: "What did the Church teach you about sex?"

"Don't talk about it or do it."

"Nothing! It's negative, denied, a sin."

"It's dark and private, and tolerated for procreation only."

"It's not discussed; it's only for having children, a no-no otherwise."

"Nothing was ever mentioned except purity."

"An evil part of one's person that has limited use: for procreation in marriage."

"Even now, years after leaving the Church, I feel so much conflict about just enjoying my body."

If any of this feels familiar, this book is for you.

THE CHURCH AS A *HUMAN* INSTITUTION

As children we were taught that nuns and priests were closer to God, and therefore in a better position to make decisions for us; and so we often took their word as Gospel. We know now that all of the men and women who made up the clergy, including the Pope, were (and are) as human as the rest of us. We were generally raised with the same set of specific standards and codes of behavior for living, as set forth in the Boston Catechism. Over the past few years I have become aware of how these standards, rigidly held and applied, have caused varying degrees of trauma and shame in the lives of millions of present and former Catholics. In researching this book, I heard many stories of pain and fear connected with an early Catholic upbringing. Sometimes these men and women allowed a deeper part of themselves to express the feelings while telling a story, often a story whose content was particularly shaming or frightening. At other times they denied holding on to disturbing features from their Catholic past, adamantly asserting that the Church has had no lasting influence on their lives. As an example, one former Catholic is now an active member of a non-Christian religious community, one which requires celibacy, rigid adherence to strict dietary rules, and disciplined silences; in spite of the obvious parallels, he had difficulty seeing the connection between his Catholic past, which he said he abhorred and despised, and his chosen present lifestyle.

The Catholic Church is and was composed of a group of fallible human beings. While interviewing people, I repeatedly heard Catholics say they remember believing that nuns and priests never went to the bathroom! This sounds laughable now; but we *were* taught that we all occupy different steps on a stairway to heaven, with nuns and priests on the higher elevations, all the way down to the "pagan babies," (whom we were to pray for) at the bottom. This view was very unfortunate, because it caused us to compare ourselves, first with one another, then with the clergy, and finally with God Himself. Did we measure up? Were we good enough? Never!

THE DYSFUNCTIONAL FAMILY CONNECTION

When we were kids, the Catholic Church acted as parents in a large dysfunctional family. Of course, "dysfunctional" is a relative term that has been thrown around a lot lately: we were all raised in families which existed somewhere on the continuum between severe dysfunction and health. In healthier families, children's opinions are heard and often acted upon. When my son cleverly pointed out the other day that I myself was doing the same thing he was getting in trouble for, I was willing to listen. In healthier families there is more flexibility and an awareness that children *teach*, and parents *learn*, as well as the other way around. Most importantly, change is acknowledged and welcomed. There is a desire to re-evaluate family rules and traditions and to discard or modify them whenever necessary, substituting newer and more evolved ways of doing things, for everyone's benefit. In *less* healthy families, there is more likely to be inflexibility, and it's harder for everyone to get what they need. Most of my Catholic clients tell me their parents never treated them in any kind of special way, yet all of them yearned for that more than anything else. The order of the day was to conform.

Like a more dysfunctional family, the Church has operated with a set of principles and rules which have dictated the conduct of its members, as a means of keeping the system intact, and this has often been to the detriment of its individual members. The fear of losing its sacred place as the historical "One, Holy, Catholic and Apostolic Church" has sometimes made it difficult for the Church to listen to its people. This position reflects the Church's belief that it was essentially Christ's special project. Many of the former Catholics I interviewed said that they perceived an attitude of philosophical elitism embedded in church teaching; and this sense of arrogance was often cited as a significant part of their decision to leave the Church; their feeling was that the Church, through its hierarchy, attempted to "lord it over" all other religions, while at the same time acting in a detached and patronizing way toward its own members.

This hierarchical structure that we are all familiar with—the

Pope, Cardinals, Bishops, Monsignors, priests, nuns, and so on—was erected centuries ago, and it follows a pattern consistent with the feudal age, when kings were the heads of countries, and were assumed to be wiser, holier, and certainly more powerful than the lords, knights and gentry, whose presumed intelligence and power decreased progressively down the hierarchy. This linear system is only able to function when those in power (the Pope or the King) get to act as *supreme rulers* by issuing edicts, making rules and essentially dictating and controlling the lives of those further down the hierarchy. It is also essential for those who ostensibly have less power (serfs, congregations) to accommodate and acknowledge the power of the main ruler. In doing so, those individuals collectively give over their personal control to those with more authority. In this way, both the ruler and the people also act as a *system*, with the ruler taking an active stance and the people taking a passive stance. In the case of the Church, the Pope has acted for centuries as the active, dominant presence while the members have taken the passive role, following directives issued by the Pope which affect each individual part of their lives, including sexual behavior, birth control, morality, family life and the work ethic in addition to spiritual matters.

In the 1960's and 1970's the system began to change, as many Americans began to question hierarchies of all kinds, from governments to those created by our own families. We began to see inter-relationships as important, and societal rules of all kinds were questioned as a result. For some of us raised in the Catholic faith this questioning of the hierarchical structure resulted in a decision to leave the Church. For others it has created the desire to change the Church from within. Essentially we decided to stop taking the passive role dictated by the old system. Also, ironically, the very freedom of thought encouraged by Vatican II gave people the motivation to refuse participation in a system that they could no longer endorse.

Time has moved on, and with it has come a myriad of possibilities about how we now want to live our lives. The options appear endless, and with each option comes a certain set of contingencies. How do we decide? What decisions are in our best interest? How do the decisions affect other people? How to choose?

CHOICEMAKING AND CHANGE

The job for the nineties, more than ever, is healing: fixing up the planet through conservation efforts, cleaning up toxic waste, recycling, and planning new ways to harness technology that will benefit us all. And of course we have to do this on a personal level too: the co-dependency movement, New Age thinking, and even traditional women's publications—all are encouraging us to dust and clean on a mental level, to look into ourselves and let go of the garbage, and release old buried thoughts and patterns of behavior that keep us stuck in the past. At the same time, we're encouraged to hold on to what "works", and finally, to decide what we want to believe about ourselves and our futures. The implication is that men and women have *control* in their lives and some—even great—capacity to effect positive change. If you stop and think about it, this is really mind-boggling! People are beginning to take responsibility for their own choices, with less tendency to become guilty or blame others if the choice results in unpleasant consequences. We just have to make the best decisions we can, with the skills and knowledge we possess at any particular time.

In relationships with others, we hear that we have a choice about how to react to those who behave in ways that hurt or offend us. We are encouraged to take responsibility for *ourselves* in these situations. A case in point: a married woman with six children is left high and dry by her adulterous husband. Years ago, the reaction of society would have been clear: scandalous behavior by husband, wife to be pitied, wife ashamed, wife resentful at husband and what fate has brought about. She might easily have become stuck in this posture, with resentment becoming a core element in her identity. These days, she's likely to go see a therapist who, while empathizing with all of her feelings, would also invite her to have a good look at her own part in creating the situation, and would help her to recognize that *she* gets to decide how long to hold on to her resentment and pain. How is she going to change *herself* so that she can be free to enjoy life more and have better relationships? How can she do that in a spirit of self-acceptance and compassion? The therapist might also say (in the nicest possible way, of course!) "When you are ready to let go of self-pity and the feeling of martyrdom, what are you going to *do about* it?"

In short, the main focus these days is on choicemaking. Gone are the old, comfortable black and white rules and conventions that have kept us all going: "women are the homemakers", "men are strong and don't eat quiche", "women don't really like sex, they just do it to keep their husbands happy," "girls aren't mechanically-minded." Everywhere we look, there are numerous exceptions to the old rules. Some men even know how to *cook* quiche, for God's sake! While it is true that there are still plenty of "black and whiters", more and more of us are changing our minds and making choices on issues that until now have been sacred and unquestionable. The bad news is that this creates a whole new set of anxieties for those of us in the "grey" camp: we're often totally confused, caught up in the clash between the old ideas and the new. A woman in the United States agrees to carry her daughter's unborn fetus. Can this be *okay*? While the black and white gang are unquestioningly clear on this one, the rest of us have to really struggle through with it, looking at the whole picture, grappling with particular issues related to the whole; and we often end up vacillating back and forth between acceptance and rejection of the various principles involved, before we eventually reach conclusions we can live with.

In the past, we had fewer choices to make. Moral values were spelt out by society, by the Church, by civic organizations, by the family. Everybody knew what was right and wrong. In the city and in the country, young and old, rich and poor, everyone had a role and for the most part everyone bowed to society's requirements in carrying out that particular role. Today, many feel that the very fabric of society is being destroyed. Maybe what is really going up in smoke is the *illusion* that the average man and woman is capable of consistently right and consistently loving behavior. In fact, most of us in the grey camp aren't even sure what "right behavior" means anymore! Perhaps we're beginning to accept ourselves as being truly *human*. Most of my clients come into therapy with the assumption that perfect wives, perfect husbands, perfect business partners, perfect churchgoers, actually exist. They compare themselves to others they know who "really have it together". I often spend time in sessions helping them understand that these images of perfection are figments of their own imaginations. These people just don't exist.

So in the past we conformed to society, and society saw itself as being guided by God. "In God We Trust" was a motto we adopted and lived by. Although people didn't always follow society's moral edicts in private, public agreement about God's law was firmly established. This God of the past—along with clear moral values, traditional family structures, commonly accepted rules—no longer works for many of us. The "old" God we created is patriarchal. He is the stern but ultimately forgiving Dad who wants to keep us in line for our own sakes. He loves us and cares for us but makes it clear that He calls the shots. If we're not happy or life is not working out for us, we need to appeal to Him on our knees. If our prayers aren't heard we either haven't tried hard enough or long enough, or we simply don't deserve it. In God's eyes, then, we are

His children. He loves us but we are Imperfect and must keep trying until we get it Right. This belief effectively keeps us in our place: we long for perfection, but we're saddled with an intrinsic understanding that perfection isn't possible despite how much we try to delude ourselves. In this view, we are dependent on God in a way that makes us impotent, as He dishes out good and bad experiences as He sees fit. We have little to say in the matter, our imperfection rendering our judgment unworthy of consideration.

Although this view of God now seems no longer useful (bearing in mind that we created it and are therefore in a position to alter it), many religious groups continue to implicitly or explicitly incorporate these messages into weekly services. Those of us who find these and other concepts of old impossible to live with often opt to discontinue all forms of contact with organized religion and spiritual development. Others let go of religion while independently exploring and enriching their own spiritual life. Some continue to attend services while interpreting certain phrases and concepts from spiritual teachings in ways which fit their own beliefs. Still others explore a variety of religious communities. Despite these adaptations, however, we often continue to act in ways which are inconsistent with these adult decisions. What do recovering Catholics have in common that could account for this?

CATHOLICS AND THE INNER CHILD

One thing we all have in common is what has been called the "Inner Child". This concept has been put forth by many recovery groups, such as Adult Children of Alcoholics, New Age groups, psychotherapists, and others. It's not a new concept by any means, but has been recently formulated in a simpler and more universal way. Simply put, the inner child is that part of ourselves (no longer conscious, but preserved completely in our unconscious, deeper minds) which holds childhood memories, learnings, and emotions intact. Children's minds are capable of great absorption and learning assimilation, particularly between birth and age 10. It is in that time frame that the child's expectations and understanding regarding the nature of the world are set in place. Children absorb information well, but are not capable of sophisticated reasoning. They are not able to tease out which ideas are unhealthy and which ideas are enriching and beneficial. Anything presented to a young child will be taken in and integrated as Truth, particularly those ideas which are repeated often by parents and other significant adults. It is as though the child's mind is a blank slate. Anything written on the slate is done with spray paint. The information will remain indelible, unless active attempts are made to remove it. The impact of our isolation is far-reaching and continues to influence us today, whether or not we continue to practice Catholicism, because Catholicism was *instilled* in us. We may no longer *intellectually* hold the beliefs that guided our childhoods, but we often continue to hold onto them in an emotional and psychological way.

At this point in the discussion, many present and former Catholics could be crying out: "Nonsense! I let go of all that negative stuff years ago." The question is: has the *child* part let the stuff go? Many Catholics let go of certain beliefs and ideas during early adulthood. These beliefs about the self and the self in relation to God no longer fit, and were often abruptly and aggressively discarded. In some cases these beliefs were intentionally replaced with newer, more self-supporting ones. For some of us, life simply moved on, and we ultimately found ourselves with political, sociological or other religious interests taking the place of previously held beliefs. The developmental goal of early adulthood is to do just that: to evaluate the teachings of childhood and to make decisions about which of these to bring into adulthood. In doing so, young adults often look to their parents, picking and choosing aspects of their parents' lives to emulate, and aspects to discard. All of this is done with an adult's mind. The child part of ourselves continues to remain dormant. Very few young adults spend time thinking about the "little kid" part of themselves at this point. They are hell-bent on getting *out* of childhood and into the exciting world of adulthood. The upshot is that the young adult, equipped with values and beliefs learned from parents and the Church, and to a greater or lesser extent altered through their own personal "filtration system", moves into society. Although he or she views life in a way that may be new and distinctive from the past, the emotional imprint and self-image of the *child* remain intact. It is important to recognize the unconscious as a storehouse of information. It is a microchip containing hundreds of thousands of pieces of data. The fact that this information may not be visible on the "screen" of one's mind in the present day does not mean it is gone. It can be accessed at any point. Sometimes these bits of information form images or patterns. Many present and former Catholics have spent time in therapy uncovering these patterns, which continue to have a real and lasting effect in present-day life, and they have been successful *in part* at changing their self-image. After a certain point, however, they seem to hit a road block in their own development, and continue to feel unhappy or anxious in their personal lives despite the therapy and possibly numerous other attempts to move beyond the generalized issues of their childhood.

The impact of the Church in our early lives is an important link in understanding this difficulty. The Church—and our parents—taught us both to love and to despise ourselves. It taught us how God felt about us. It taught us who to know, where to go, how to act, and how to change. The Catholic Church was a mother and father to us and *to our parents* as well. It was the ultimate authority, as good as God. If we needed help, it provided for our needs. We were dependent on the Church for our feelings of safety and well-being. A survey respondent said this:

"I didn't have any trouble realizing, after 25 years of marriage and with a divorce pending, that I needed to sort out which of my beliefs came from being the 'accommodating wife', going along with my husband's views about politics, business, and the rest, and which beliefs were my own. What surprised me was a sudden awareness further down the line that the Church had exerted that same type of influence, and I had gone along with it for just as many years and more. I had traded in my own ability to think and feel for the security the Church provided. I no longer feel I can afford the high price I've been paying."

For many of us, guilt was the controlling power that motivated us to "keep our slate clean". We were keenly aware of the kinds of actions that the Church frowned on. We were taught that our spiritual well-being came from following God's plan as interpreted by the Church. Our task was to carefully scrutinize ourselves and look for error and potential for error. In this way the Church itself remained "pure", while individual members remained "tainted". Part of the way in which this has been maintained is through the concept of Papal Infallibility.

PAPAL INFALLIBILITY

Papal Infallibility, of course, is the concept that allows the Pope, when he chooses to exercise this capacity in serious matters, to act as God's direct representative. This does not mean that anything the Pope says is the "Word of God", but that he has access to divinely inspired information whenever necessary. The concept of papal infallibility did not start with Peter as many people might assume, but was first developed in the 14th century by a theologian named Guido Terreni. Since then there has been much controversy about it within theological circles. It has only been in recent years, however, that lay people have begun to question it. Despite the fact that Papal Infallibility was to be used in regard to serious issues only, it has often been assumed that *anything* the Pope had to say was a representation of God's word; and as representatives of the Vatican, the clergy in our neighborhoods acted as spiritual guides, spreading the Pope's message in matters of faith. The Church itself did not seem to be concerned with correcting the misunderstanding of some of its people regarding Infallibility, understandably. What power! And with that power came the message that the Church acted as God's sole, anointed representative, emphasizing its own authority and our insignificance. As such, many former Catholics live in a perpetual state of low-level depression, having an inner child who says "I'll never be good enough for God. I keep making mistakes. I'll never get to heaven. Why try?" Many of us walk around with feelings of depression, anger, shame and fear, originating in our earliest years. I remember the terror I experienced when Sister J. stood above me in math class, masterfully infusing me with the fear of God. My adult self no longer fears nuns, but this often gets transferred in weird ways: for example, I might find myself feeling anxious or blanking out when I have to handle a difficult transaction at the bank, as though good old Sister J. has returned in the form of a bank teller! The child part remembers, and in her concrete and unsophisticated way, assumes she may be shamed. The threat of eternal pain and suffering was always present, and created an intensity and penetrating chill that had a life of its own.

The control the Church exerted over us as children took many forms. The next chapter will focus on *sin*, and the ways in which this concept has negatively impacted us.

CHAPTER TWO

SIN

"Believing in You, I feel my nothingness.
I know that I am a sinner.
So often have I offended You.
You have forgiven numberless offences.
Now I fall before You.
May my lowliness and nothingness
Draw Your eyes towards me!"

*Taken from a pamphlet entitled
'Christ Within My Heart.'*

All of mankind's problems, according to traditional Catholic doctrine, emanated from Original Sin. The main idea, as you remember, is that God bestowed all kinds of gifts on Adam and Eve, the original dysfunctional parents. After God gave Adam and Eve their gifts, He then tested them by commanding them not to eat from a certain tree, the tree of Good and Evil. The injunction *not* to eat from this tree always bothered me in this context, because it portrays a parental God: parental in a particularly human and limited way, as though He needed to exercise this kind of power over us in order to feel good about Himself. We are *not* to get into the cookie jar, *not* to forget to pay our taxes, *not* to say naughty words. Could an all-giving force really be so negatively focused? As the story continues, they were then tempted by the Devil (in serpent's clothing) to eat the forbidden apple anyway. Eve then encouraged Adam to do so, and the rest is history. As a child I always had a lot of trouble with this whole thing. The fact that I began in later life to see it as myth, as a metaphor, did nothing to help my discomfort. First of all, if God created men in His own image, how could we be even capable of thinking and doing naughty things? Free will or no free will, if a baby shoot comes out of a flower it stays a flower, it doesn't turn into a turnip. If we come from God, we have God-like qualities. The interpretation the Church espoused was that we came into the world as rotten apples, that we continue to be gnawed at by worms, and that only a very select few will be mysteriously transformed into wholesome fruit, chosen for the harvest. Perhaps this was a well-intentioned effort on the part of the Church to motivate its members and to lead them towards the light; however, modern psychology has taught us that guilt, fear and shame are poor motivators, more likely to result in behaviors that hurt the self and others.

One survey responder had developed a more evolved interpretation of the myth: that Adam and Eve were so bowled over by the awareness of their own magnificence that they forgot to keep in mind the fact that they were parts of a larger, even more magnificent whole. It is as though we all have amnesia and have forgotten the essence of who we are. It is the *act of forgetting* that creates problems in our lives, *not* the fact that we are rotten to the core. Although I think it's realistic for mankind to take responsibility for losing its way, I have a problem with the idea inherent in the Adam and Eve story, of God *testing* them, to see if they would blow it. This never seemed fair to me. After all, they hadn't even gotten their feet wet in the Garden of Eden, then, wham, a test! Again, I can't see God coercing anyone to fail, and yet we all behave as if the story were true, all of us waiting for God to get mad, to inflict some type of disaster on us, in a personal and vindictive way. I remember thinking (even though I knew I'd have to go to Confession for it) that God seemed pretty mean to shut them out that way, to withdraw His gifts and friendship. For most of us, the image of an angry, punitive father began here. It is also here that we learned to feel shame. Here, for example, is Bob:

"One Good Friday, when I was a painfully shy 16 year-old, I was sitting through one of those mega-services that I think lasted three hours, at least. Halfway through I had to slip out for a bathroom break, and there all of a sudden was Julie, the secret Love of my Life, with no-one else around! I stole two blissful, innocent minutes of private conversation with her, only to be discovered by Father Flynn (why had *he* slipped out?) who looked down at me with utter disdain and said, 'Robert, couldn't you have picked a less holy occasion to practice your idle flirtations? Get back in the church.' I was mortified and deeply ashamed, and still feel it today, as ridiculous as that sounds."

I wondered how other recovering Catholics viewed Original Sin, so I asked survey responders to offer ideas which reflected both their past and their present thinking on the subject. Here is a sampling of their responses:

PAST	PRESENT
As a child I knew that Adam and Eve disobeyed, which has hurt everyone since it gives each of us a bad proclivity from the beginning.	A reprehensible document spawned by malevolent priests.
I thought it meant I was a bad person from birth.	Original *Guilt*. Original power for the Church.
I believed Adam and Eve were real.	Man was simply disobedient in some way.
Human beings' sinful nature is explained by Adam and Eve. I felt like it was supposed to be redeemed by Jesus, so it was irrelevant.	A counter-productive way of explaining human nature.

Eve's role has always posed problems for me too. I have to admit that I am rather curious about the sex of the writer of Genesis. It wouldn't surprise me a bit to learn that he was a male. Although many individuals no longer take the Adam and Eve story literally, the fact remains that hundreds of generations before us have believed it and have unconsciously accepted the assumption that women are guilty by association: the theme of women leading men astray is deeply embedded in our culture. The other theme which has had obvious long-term ramifications is that of Eve having been born of Adam, a second thought on God's part, created as a "helpmate". In an age where millions of single-parent women are learning to care for themselves, such an idea is now inadequate. Even the concept of God as male is outdated. The implications of holding on to these ideas, in either a conscious or unconscious way, are great for all past or present Judeo-Christians. Many couple relationships are falling apart in our day and age, and many individuals in past generations simply tolerated their spouses until death parted them. Reinterpreting or letting go of the Adam and Eve story provides an excellent way of moving us past the spirit of subtle blame and intolerance that has characterized preceding generations.

To really understand Original Sin, it is necessary to look at the historical roots of this teaching. Many Catholics were never taught that the concept of Original Sin as we know it came out of the writing of St. Augustine, in the 5th century. Augustine's doctrine of Original Sin differed greatly from the view of other theologians of his time. While his contemporaries saw man as essentially good, but able to exercise free will, Augustine believed the will of mankind to be fully controlled by the power of sin. As such, those whom God chose to bless would "make it" into heaven, while those who were not blessed went to hell. Augustine's teachings were later adopted by the Council of Trent, which issued edicts declaring that mankind is guilty of Original Sin, having descended from Adam, and that all subsequent generations would also inherit this guilt, which could only be removed by Baptism.

In recent years, some authorities within the Church have liberalized their teaching on Original Sin, perhaps spurred on by increasingly accurate scientific information regarding the origin of the species, which doesn't allow for a simple explanation of the beginning of mankind. Although this movement away from the old concepts of Original Sin may be a positive development for the Church, I am more aware of the continued significance of the past teaching in the lives of countless individuals. Many times

I have sat in my therapy office, hearing stories of pain and misery in families, stories which have been repeated in generation after generation: stories of alcoholism, sexual abuse, violence, emotional abuse, and illness; and I have been able to trace this back to their long-standing conviction of their own innate worthlessness. It is my impression that this particular belief needs to be thrown in the garbage or petrified, as an ancient relic which no longer serves the common good (if it ever did).

One metaphor for understanding our ability to disconnect from our creative purpose, or God, or whatever term you choose, is the idea of getting lost in the forest. We have a map that we made, and a lot of the directions on the map are accurate and get us where we want to go. Sometimes, though, the map tells us to go down a road that dead ends. "The map has to be right", we say. We backtrack and try again and again, until we finally realize that we either need help in reading the map, or that it was inaccurate to begin with. In the meantime, though, we've endured sore feet, we've gotten irritated at our companions, we've found we are out of food, and we're feeling tired and confused. The Original Sin method would encourage us to beat ourselves up for having gotten lost in the first place. Being away from our home camp means that sometimes we are going to draw faulty maps, sometimes accurate maps. Part of the job is to learn which is which. This can only be done in a spirit of great compassion and tolerance, both for oneself and for one's travelling companions. I believe that *all* human action is essentially an attempt to do what will be of the most benefit based on what the individual knows and understands at the time. This is not to say, for example, that joining a Satanic cult is going to be for anyone's highest good. Bizarre as it may sound, however, those who commit even the most heinous crimes are acting out of *what they believe to be* their highest good. This does not mean that society will not or should not have a say in this, or may not need at times to exercise control over behavior that is dangerous to the self or others. But it seems essential to me that we find ways of recognizing what is going on in that person's mind.

One way of doing this is to use what I call the "videotape technique". When you have trouble understanding why someone is behaving in a way that just makes no sense, sit back in a chair and pretend you are watching a videotape of that person's life, from the moment they are born. Try to imagine how that person could be doing what he is now doing, and have it make sense; because if we only have enough data, it *will* make sense. It doesn't mean that you will necessarily agree with his behavior, but you will suddenly *get it*. It is this process of getting it that will make or break us as a culture. If you believe that suffering, illness, war, and disease are unavoidable, you will, day by day, create the atmosphere necessary for these things to flourish. The Original Sin concept encourages us to see these as punishments, not as learning devices. If we didn't feel so guilty, our lives would necessarily work better.

Again, the answer seems clear. We need to un-learn, to let go of the idea of Original Sin, not only in our adult minds, but in our inner, deeper child mind. To do this is to conscientiously, consistently, and mindfully give our primary attention to our *successes*, and gratefully acknowledge all the effort that went into creating them, while letting go of the word *mistake*, and replacing it with words like effort, try, attempt. What about all of those hundreds of baskets Michael Jordan *didn't* get in while he was learning to play basketball? Were those mistakes? Most of us would say of course not, they were necessary learning steps along the way. However it's not quite so easy to view a 15 year- old drug seller's attempts as anything other than mistakes. But what could be really going on here? What is the 15 year-old after? He's after money, which he thinks will make him happy, and which will make other people in the neighborhood like him and look up to him. Isn't this an attempt to take a road to success? It will probably not pan out, and he will have to regroup time and again as he re-checks his "map", but it's up to him to decide he wants to take a different road. It's our job to protect ourselves, perhaps, so that we don't get hurt in the process and so our children don't get taken down the road with him, but it seems essential that we don't disrespect him, however we may choose to respond to his behavior, that we appreciate what we can about him, even though we may be travelling down a different path.

The Adam and Eve story taught us to see the 15 year-old in very black and white terms. The story encourages a dualistic mentality: "all or nothing", "perfect or imperfect", "right or wrong", "good or bad". It teaches us that perfection is the only way, that we essentially blew it in God's eyes. Like the Genesis writer, we all love to find someone else to put the blame on. Very few of us are satisfied with ourselves if we do less than a perfect job, yet the pain of imperfection is so great that we either throw it onto others who *seem* different from us, or we berate ourselves mercilessly. Most of us were raised in families that propagated the idea of perfection above all else. Many of us were also raised in families that had difficulty recognizing the specialness of each individual member. Often, this resulted in unique talents and abilities going to waste. In some cases the parents of these children noticed these talents and decided not to acknowledge them, so the child wouldn't "get a big head". As a result, the kids grew into adulthood without any essential understanding of who they were. The parents in question were simply following a time-honored pattern. In order to maintain the good/bad dualism of the Adam and Eve tradition, good behavior and personal characteristics must always play second fiddle to imperfection. If there is one scrap of imperfection in the child, that imperfection looms over positive traits and characteristics, just as Adam and Eve's mistake loomed in our minds over any positive traits and attributes they possessed. I think the idea here is simple. We keep pushing, prodding, and looking for what is wrong in ourselves and others, until we earn our way back; until we get it *right*. We learned this from our parents and from their parents and, in my opinion, it just doesn't work. This doesn't mean that we don't have anything to improve or to change in life. What no longer works is the original premise: that we are "bad", that the process of life centers on the need to keep our "badness" in front of our minds, hour after hour, day after day like a guard following us around in an open prison. This quotation from a Catholic pamphlet of the 1930's speaks to this tendency:

"My sins are ever before my eyes. There have been so many of them, and they were so grievous, so shameful, so full of ingratitude. Often I have committed them at times when grace spoke most powerfully. And how often have I not broken my resolutions! How often have I not fallen again a short time after forgiveness.

"O dear Lord, though I have abused Your patience, scorned your mercy, though I am unworthy of being forgiven, yet in Your presence I feel keenly, and want to feel still more deeply, sorrow for my offences. I am sorry because I have deserved endless torments of hell. I am sorry still more because I have wounded the love of a Friend. Had I acted towards a beloved benefactor with the same ingratitude, I should not dare to ask forgiveness.

"With the help of Your grace I trust I shall never fall again. I shall shun the dangerous occasions which in the past have brought about my downfall. I shall avoid persons, objects, places and circumstances, which cause me to sin."

The problem was that we just couldn't deliver. We couldn't avoid persons, objects, and circumstances which caused us to sin! And every time we screwed up we broke a promise that wasn't possible in the first place. As one recovering Catholic put it:

"As a kid I was always scared because I had either just committed a sin or was about to; I really hate the word sin. It has a lot of negative associations. I'd like to take it out of the dictionary because no matter how it's *interpreted* it leaves a bad taste in my mouth."

The pamphlet continues:

"And yet, O merciful Lord, while I am taking this resolve, I cannot forget that I have taken it so often, and broken it time and again. Look down upon my infirmity. May my sorrow be pleasing unto You. May it win forgiveness for all my sins. Cleanse my heart, O Lord, that I may become more worthy of You."

How did this type of influence effect our own thinking, and how does it impact the way in which we may continue to see our relationships? The following narrative by one interviewee provides some honest and courageous insights.

"I feel like I'm living a sham of a life, just waiting for someone to find me out. This has manifested itself in my relationships with others. I am constantly in awe of my friendships. I have some remarkable people for friends, yet I question why they *are* my friends. Objectively, I can list my qualities and work hard at being a loyal and supportive person in their lives. Frustratingly, I still live with the suspicion that 'If you really knew me, you wouldn't like me'. I have been in therapy and also worked in a men's group for two and a half years. For all the disclosure, sharing, and accepting of problems of others, I persist in harboring feelings of unworthiness. I am sure that, at least in part, this feeling was fostered by a Church that told me I was stained from birth with Original Sin. There was nothing I could do to prevent that. There was nothing I could do on my own to rid myself of that sin. God alone could do that at His whim. This God was not an easily forgiving guy, from my education. He wanted us to be Christlike (read 'Perfect'). There was just no way to do that. As a child I could not get through the week without racking up a bunch of sins to tell the priest about. More stains. And only the priest's word for it that the stains were gone *if* I were truly repentant, and who knows if I'm repenting well enough!"

What is the cure for our seemingly innate tendency to chide and punish ourselves hour after hour and day after day? Again, the answer seems to be to simply spend hour after hour, day after day acknowledging successes, large and small, in both ourselves and others. People sometimes call this a "positive mental attitude". Personally, this has always sounded Pollyanna-ish to me. People with positive mental attitudes go around smiling a lot and offering good cheer, and seem generally larger than life. Many of us raised to see only black and white feel like we can't compete with these people, so we don't even try. I think there are numerous other ways to find success in the self and in others, as many ways as there are individual human beings. Some of these ways are demonstrated very quietly. If you find yourself going through the grocery store privately noting all of the strange, weird, and bizarre people there and making judgments about them, try instead to silently and warmly acknowledge the successes of those same people. The fact that their areas of development may be different from yours is totally irrelevant, just the outer trappings. Forget the clothes, the hair style, the dirt, the makeup, the bloodshot eyes, the fur coat, the ragged coat. Focus on finding something about them that you can respect and like. The more successfully you do this towards others, the more you will treat *yourself* this way too.

It is up to you, therefore, to decide if you want to see yourself and the other person as the Devil, or if you want to assign him (and therefore, yourself) the Adam and Eve roles: roles which place blame on one another as a means of alleviating personal feelings of guilt, roles which are circular and never-ending, roles where there is no winner, only two losers. The only solution is to re-educate the kid part of ourselves, and provide a more healthy view of ourselves in relation to God. Whether we believe in God or not, this re-education is going to be more nurturing than some of what we were taught. Maybe nobody "up there" is mad at us. Maybe we're just mad at *ourselves*, and need to stop!

IDENTIFY DON'T COMPARE

One way we can change our point of view is to let go of the need to make comparisons, the tendency to see ourselves as the only Adam and Eve on the block: either by thinking everyone else has succeeded in life, where we have failed, or, conversely, thinking we have it made. Comparisons are unnecessary because each of us is unique. Spending time looking at differences enhances feelings of isolation and guilt, whether you see yourself as top dog or on the bottom of the pile.

Another unfortunate influence of the Genesis tale relates to avoidance, procrastination and uncertainty. We avoid doing what we need to do in order to succeed, then get mad at ourselves for our lack of motivation. Sometimes the clear indication that success is available to us (simply through studying, or hard work, for example) causes anxiety. We are about to do well, and that doesn't fit with the old Adam and Eve story at all, because it would mean actually enjoying the Garden of Eden and feeling good, so we do something to goof things up once again. Feeling depressed may not be ideal, but it is often more desirable than the feeling of uncertainty that comes with the fear that we may be okay after all! Perhaps this is the appeal of the Dracula theme: when the light starts to come in, we need to protect ourselves.

One respondent had this to say:

> "When I look at what it is about me that isn't healthy, I see predominantly a feeling of unworthiness, guilt, and a vague depression constantly beneath the surface of my other feelings. These feelings have arisen in many facets of my life. In studies when I was in school and now, in the workplace, I always have felt the need to be perfect. The bright side to that was and is that I generally produce good grades or work. The dark side is that I never feel *really good* about it because, of course, it isn't, and can't be, perfect. I find it difficult to take criticism because I'm already feeling vulnerable. But what is worse, I cannot accept praise for my work because I know it's not really good enough (and besides, pride is a sin, right?!)"

The concept of sin has created untold amounts of fear, guilt, and anxiety. While the Catholic Church was by no means alone in using fear as a means of attempting to motivate people, it did demonstrate a particular "brand" of motivation through the concepts of mortal and venial sin.

MORTAL SIN

Mortal sin was serious sin. We were taught that God would be very unhappy with the individual if he or she knowingly acted against specific laws of the Church. The Church decided what God saw as serious and told millions of people that they would go to hell if they did not follow the Church's requirements. Examples of mortal sin included: eating less than three hours before going to Communion, intentionally eating meat on Friday, and having sexual relations before marriage or outside of marriage. The Church essentially told us how God thought and what God felt on these and numerous other issues. Many survey respondents said they felt confused as children, wondering how God could be so angry, and felt fearful of making a wrong move that would land them in hell if they died before going to Confession. This was a very real concern to many children. Imagine yourself, as a 7 year- old child, being told that you would go to Hell, where you would burn in horrible pain forever, if you knowingly ate meat on Friday! As we have said, small children absorb all they hear as truth. I remember sitting in Church after Communion in a state of sheer and utter panic, trying to remember if I had fasted the prescribed number of hours. One survey respondent described it in this way:

"The other power the Church had was fear, incredible fear. You go astray, and you are going to spend the rest of time—not tomorrow, not the rest of your life, but the rest of *time*—suffering unnameable pains. The nuns loved to describe hell as pain beyond any pain. Imagine a fire, they said, burning over your entire body forever. They said that didn't come *close* to describing the pain you will feel. And you say that to someone and they say 'You didn't believe that, did you?' Yes, I *did* believe that! I had no other choice. I believed it as much as I believe there is a table right there. I was dreadfully afraid of doing anything wrong. I was taught that if a random sexual thought entered my head and I entertained it for a millisecond, I was headed for eternal damnation, and I believed it. Not that you're going to get hit by someone, not that someone's going to yell at you, you know those are fearful things for a child, but that it's possible (if lightening hit you right then) that you're going to spend the rest of immortal time in hell. I don't think I'm overstating it. I was terrified."

VENIAL SIN

Venial sin, on the other hand, was seen as "common sin", and it made up the content of the Saturday confessional. Many respondents said they made up sins to tell in Confession. They also described Confession as "scary" and "humiliating". One recovering Catholic said she could not think of any sins to tell and was shamed by a sister for this in front of other students. Another said she remembered being petrified, waiting to make her first Confession, while a stern-faced sister patrolled the line. She had to come out of the Confession because she couldn't remember the words, and was shamed for this. One interviewee had the following to say about venial sin and Confession:

"Venial sin. Ya! Those were the ones you could do! What the hell! I enjoyed venial sins. That was the thing about Confession. Just make up a few venials and that seemed to take care of it. It makes me laugh, these classifications about sin! I'd stay clear of the mortals, though. I'd take that pretty seriously."

Here are some excerpts taken from survey questionnaires on the subject of sin. Again, the comments on the left indicate the responders thoughts and feelings about sin as a child, while the comments on the right reflect their thoughts and feelings as adults. While Confession was touted, even then, as the primary

PAST	PRESENT
A bad deed that marks one's soul indelibly and dooms one to Hell. Can only be erased by absolution in Confession. It seemed harsh. *(Mortal)* Minor wrongdoings that sully one's soul but that can be erased by prayer, etc. I figured I had more than my share since almost everything was sinful. *(Venial)*.	So there are bad deeds and bad people. Who's to say when some wrongdoing is venial not mortal? It's relative and mistakes are a learning process. Some people can be inherently evil in their unwillingness to learn, but one need ask what it is that *makes* them unwilling. "Judge not..."
There are bad sins and really bad sins. If you died with a mortal sin on your soul, you go to hell.	Acquiescing to human weakness. The Church graded degrees of misbehavior.
Very important in growing up. Confession was a great fear.	I don't believe in rating evil. We're all a mixture of good and evil.
Didn't make any sense to me.	Still doesn't make any sense.
Mortal? Never did one. Venial? I made 'em up.	Sin is hurting yourself.
Violations of the Commandments, willful forsaking of God.	Not relevant in the absolute cosmic sense, and not the best way to proscribe behavior.
Serious and minor offenses.	Oversimplified explanations of good and evil.

> I was always scared because I knew I had just committed a sin or was about to—never enjoyed my childhood.

> I really hate this word. It has a lot of negative associations. I'd like to take it out of the dictionary because no matter how it's *interpreted* it leaves a bad taste in my mouth.

method for releasing us from sin, the emphasis for many of us seems not to have been on release, but on the *experience* of guilt and shame. Penance was the means of punishment for sin. For some, leaving the Confessional with a "clean soul" was emotionally refreshing. For others, however, this wasn't a feeling of true cleansing, but a sense of gratitude that we were no longer in that dark little box, feeling shame and fear. The difficulty, of course, is that our humanity meant that we would start to sin again the second we left the Confessional. How refreshing it would have been to have been told that doing things we are not proud of can be a way of learning and growth.

Unfortunately, many of us who attended Catholic grade schools received little help in understanding the world in which we lived. Most Catholic schools were staffed primarily by nuns until the 60's when more lay teachers joined their ranks. Many survey respondents described nuns as angry, strict, and often spiteful disciplinarians, acting more like Policewomen of the Soul than nurturing teachers and guides, with a main job requirement focused on searching and routing out any and all error so that we could remain "pure in Spirit".

Between the fear of what would happen to us in the future if we committed mortal sin, and the fear of the Confessional and the clergy in the present if we committed venial sin, a state of anxiety was with us constantly, to a greater or lesser extent throughout most of our childhoods. Because we were good little children, many of us struggled incessantly to keep our slate clean, trying harder and harder to achieve an unreachable state of perfection totally impossible on the human plane. Often, we were unaware we were "in error" and never understood the thinking behind the reactions of the clergy or our parents. This seems particularly true for children who got into trouble a lot. These children, shamed often, and often physically abused in the classroom, report as adults that they simply "gave up" after a certain amount of humiliation.

One client described spending an entire school year sitting outside the classroom on the floor, as punishment for his behavior. I also remember this happening to several children at my school. This same client also recalled being made to scrape his knuckles against the stucco wall of the school until his fingers bled, as a punishment. All of us, whether we were "good" children or "bad" children, experienced the feeling that we were unworthy. One Catholic who now attends other churches as well as the Catholic Church, told this story:

"I remember when I was 7 or 8 having marched in a procession in Church, and having received Communion. We went back to our classrooms to eat breakfast. I started to drink my orange juice and the nun came bearing down on me. She shouted that I should be talking to Jesus and slapped my hand. I never forgot it".

Another former Catholic remembered sitting in a classroom when he was eight years old after Mass. His teacher sternly asked a little girl why she hadn't gone to Communion. The girl said "Because I have a mortal sin on my soul." This man said he had carried the remembrance of her look of humiliation, coupled with his feeling of compassion, into his adult life. "Imagine an eight year old living with that kind of fear", he said.

This type of event created considerable confusion and conflict in the minds of many Catholic children. We were encouraged to be loving and patient, and yet the very same individuals who were teaching us to be loving and patient often did not demonstrate those same qualities. We were taught that hurting our brother was a sin and yet many Catholic children saw some form of violence daily, aimed at themselves, or a sibling, or a classmate.

In retrospect, we can assume that the belief in "Satan and his works" contributed to our teachers' focus on sin and its renunciation. As Catholics, we were taught that the chief instigator of sin was the Devil. In the same way that many of us pictured God as a man with a long, grey beard, the Devil was red and carried a pitchfork. This image was instilled in our minds at an early age. Often, our expectations of both God and the Devil were the same. Satan was angry and demanding, and so was God, particularly when represented by nuns or priests who were angry or violent. Many reported having had fearful fantasies about the Devil, which may have had the effect of controlling their behavior, but at a great personal price. I interviewed a number of people whose grown-up faces betrayed sudden looks of fear when the Devil was mentioned. Often, these individuals went on to tell a personal experience from their childhood in a humorous or lighthearted way; but the momentary look of fear betrayed a frightened internal response; and in this way, the child part of them would continue to experience undue guilt, shame and fear, whether triggered by recollections from the past or by present day events. Here are two examples:

"When I was in first grade we were told that our guardian angel sat on our right shoulder and Satan sat on our left shoulder, and they battled each other for our souls. I was left-handed, and Sister C. associated this with Satan, so she would make me put my left hand on my desk and take my own ruler with my right hand and slap myself with it. Then I had to put my left hand behind my back and pick up my pen or pencil with my right hand and practice writing with it. I couldn't do it. It was so embarrassing because the rest of the class would be doing something else the whole time. My hand would get so red after a while but I didn't know how to tell my parents—I didn't know how to phrase it. Eventually, my mom noticed it and dealt with it with the school and it stopped happening.

"The idea of Satan has always been really fearful because of all of that. When I was in high school I went to see *The Exorcist* and I had such fear. I really believed all of that as a child. All of my friends were laughing the whole time. Periodically, the fear of Satan comes into play in my life, and I connect it with that whole idea of Satan on my shoulder."

Another former Catholic described Satan in this way:

"We were taught that he was the greatest angel, but that he got too big of an ego and wanted to be in charge of heaven and was defeated by St. Michael and cast into permanent fires of damnation, where he dedicates his energy to stealing souls from God. I remember it scared the daylights out of me. My Irish grandmother told me that if I stared at myself in the mirror too much I'd see the Devil looking back at me one day. To this day I still don't like to look in the mirror!"

The concepts of guilt and sin seem directly tied to many of the woes we experience as humans. There are various ways in which we psychologically manage these internal feelings of shame: we can attempt to deny their existence (often becoming physically ill as a result); we can project them onto others (thereby creating mistrust, chaos and hostility in our relationships and in the larger world around us); or we can endlessly explore and examine them (often becoming self-obsessed, without ever achieving peace of mind). The message we were implicitly or explicitly given was that we were either being Perfectly Good or we were Wicked; and because not many of us were able to sustain being Perfectly Good (except on rare occasions!) that meant that we got to be Wicked, a lot. Perhaps the truth is that we are all screwed up *and* we are all Divine (whatever that may mean to you). The being screwed up is simply a forgetting of our divinity, no more, no less. New Age writers assure us that we are truly divine; while I believe this on an ultimate spiritual level, on a practical one it is often less than helpful. I prefer seeing us as a mixed bag, ultimately divine, but living with fears and shortcomings that are normal for this day and age, and need to be worked with, rather than glossed over with crystals, tarot cards, and other outer trappings which may be a "quick fix" but do nothing to deal with the larger issues. Many of us recovering Catholics continue to expect punishment (or dish it out to ourselves, knowingly or unknowingly); but punishment will never move us forwards, and neither will a naive reliance on easy answers. Instead we must become committed to a process of integrating our disparate and contradictory parts, a process that requires patience, compassion, dedication and love.

CHAPTER THREE

THE BODY

rowing up Catholic, we received many mixed messages relating to the body. As young children, we fully absorbed these messages into our minds. When obvious inconsistencies became apparent, and we started asking questions, many of us were given pat answers that did not satisfy our natural curiosity. An aura of secrecy and shame often accompanied these answers. Some of us sensed this secrecy and shame particularly whenever body subjects were involved, and we went underground, choosing to avoid questions altogether. Sometimes the body was portrayed by our teachers as holy and beatific, while at other times it was denigrated. One particularly mixed message related to what would happen to the body after death. The basic idea was that we would be reunited with our bodies in heaven. This message emphasized the notion that bodies are worth hanging onto after death, to be "glorified" at the time of the Last Judgment. This glorified body would not hurt, suffer, or be subjected to base needs (for food, water, sex, or elimination). Even though all of this was to happen in the future, in heaven, we were instructed to think and pray about this in the present. The hidden conflictual message was that the human body and its functions are inferior to the "heavenly body" described above. One survey respondent described his own confusion this way:

> "We were taught that the soul and the body would be reunited on the Last Day. This confused me. What if you died in a fire or had been blown up? Did your soul join with ashes or gore? If your body was somehow magically reconstituted, then why was cremation wrong? As an adult, the whole idea of resurrection of the body seems an unspiritual attachment to the physical world. Why would a spirit want to be encumbered by a body?"

Denial of the body was demonstrated by the many ways in which both actual suffering and the symbolic infliction of suffering were venerated by the Church. Catholic children for many generations were required to fast for long periods before receiving Communion, the physical body's needs taking second position to the presumed needs of the Spirit. In many grade school classrooms children were required to sit for long periods if one child misbehaved, and many children received bizarre and unnecessary punishments that involved physical pain and discomfort. Much of this seemed patterned after the lives of the Saints. Those Saints who were martyred were seen to be particularly holy, and therefore to be emulated. Again, conflictual messages abounded. The body, we were told, is the temple of the Holy Spirit, and yet we were implicitly taught that it was also a vessel to be abused: that sadism and masochism are acceptable, as demonstrated by the teachings and functioning of our own classrooms.

Here is an example of how these teachings may continue to effect our adult lives:

"Even now, years after leaving the Church, I feel so much conflict about just enjoying my body. If I'm sick, although I hate to admit it, I feel properly punished for whatever is going on in my life at the time. This is a subtle thing, but a thing I learned in the Church. Just saying 'Don't be so silly, forget that stuff' doesn't magically take it away. I'm always having to fight the 'love of suffering.' This is *also* embarrassing to admit, but I can be sick, and when my husband comes in I'll pretend to be sicker than I am, I'll get into the role, you know. I remember being a kid and pretending to be a Saint dying. It's the same kind of thing, really...."

Another respondent provided these insights:

"The very first thing I learned about was Adam and Eve and how their having knowledge made them ashamed of their bodies, and how they needed to cover them up. I was *supposed* to be ashamed of my body. It was, somehow, not good. (But if we were made in God's image...?) This set up a conflict for me. Here we had this body that we were supposed to be ashamed of. However, this was the temple of my soul and I should never defile it. I should care for it and keep it clean and pure and healthy! Then why was I supposed to be ashamed of it? Since my questions were unanswerable, my feelings of guilt won out and I was ashamed. Once again, I would never have a 'Perfect Body' and I was again guilty, another stain on my soul. To add to that bodily confusion were stories from the Church of people suffering physically for God. People fasting for days, deliberately disfiguring themselves, inflicting pain on themselves for God and taking tortures and death for God."

Another conflictual message is related to the phrase "Body of Christ". Much emphasis in this century has been placed on the

Eucharistic meal, which is described as "the Body and Blood of Christ". As Catholics we were raised to believe that the host was mystically transformed into Christ's body (Transubstantiation). Our Protestant friends saw this as confusing, frightening and strange, to say the least. I do not intend to get into a discussion of doctrine here, but I do want to emphasize the conflictual messages present. We had already learned that the body was "not worthy", and yet Christ's body was magical, mystical, and somehow essential to the process of spiritual renewal offered through the Eucharist. The confusion which arose for many of us was often reinforced by and combined with the shame we received from clergy or from our parents, alluding to the idea that we might not be "good enough" or "clean enough" to receive the host. Several respondents told stories of having been roughly pulled out of a Communion line when a sister observed that he or she hadn't been to Confession that week. Others mentioned the fear of accidently chewing the host.

To some extent, we need to acknowledge the fact that we were young, and unable to think in abstract terms; instead we tended to think concretely and to accept what we were told at face value. The difficulty for some of us came in later adolescence or adulthood, when we looked at what the Church told us to believe, and still didn't get it. In addition, many of the beliefs, mores and traditions of the Church were developed centuries ago, in an effort to speak to simple peasant people in a way which allowed the greatest degree of control over their lives, at a time in which the Church was all-powerful. Today we have become far better educated, and less willing to accept pat answers, like "it's a question of faith", as a response to complex life issues; instead we are increasingly recognizing the value of talking, delving, discussing, and working on developing fruitful lives in the face of ambiguity and complexity. Here, for example, are the words of one of my clients:

"One day I was in a coffeehouse and talking to a really nice priest. Things were going well until I started questioning a few things; just opening up some religious discussion, mainly about sexuality. Somewhere along the line I became aware of this look that felt patronizing, although he was smiling the whole time. I was really aware, even then, that I was feeling embarrassed and ashamed and that he would have an argument for anything I happened to say. I have had the same feeling since then on the one or two occasions when I've gotten into religion with Jehovah's Witnesses at the front door. Come to think of it, that would be pretty interesting, watching a debate between a Jehovah's Witness and a Jesuit. *Now* I feel really comfortable with my own beliefs. I also know that I could feel shamed in any kind of Catholic setting, so I tend to steer clear of that."

We all felt some degree of confusion about the body. In addition to a general feeling of discomfort and lack of clarity, boys and girls were given separate messages particularly directed to them. What were girls taught about their bodies, either directly or indirectly? What were boys taught?

GIRLS AND THEIR BODIES

The Virgin Mary and the Virgin Birth

For Catholic girls, the Virgin Mary was the primary role model. A statue of Mary had a place in every Catholic Church. Emphasis on saying the Rosary, May Day crowning of Mary, and praying to Mary were all part of Catholic life. In some families a little altar to Mary was put up as a place to pray. Nuns dressed in clothing resembling Mary's. We were all encouraged to devote ourselves to Mary. Above all else, Mary was the symbol of purity.

This emanates from the teaching that she was born of the Immaculate Conception. These two words were used in capital letters, to emphasize their significance. We were taught that Jesus was not conceived "in the usual way" (although the usual way was not named or described in religion class) but that God mystically impregnated Mary. It should be noted that the idea of the Virgin birth is another concept that theologians argue about. For most of us growing up in this century, however, the Virgin birth concept was not simply an idea, but a reality.

Below are comments from the questionnaire in relation to Mary. The sex of the respondent is indicated, as well.

PAST	PRESENT
Mary was the mother of God/ Jesus. Never sinned. Had a "tough" role assigned—very *holy!* (F)	Reject! Not a virgin—a myth created by the Church for power reasons.
Chosen by God, magically fertilized by God without sex. Gave birth to Jesus. (F)	Unlikely that anyone gave birth without insemination.
Giggled about what the Holy Ghost had done. Also admiration for stepping on the snake. (F)	Not important.
The perfect woman/mother. (M)	An appeasement to the goddess-worshipping tribes being absorbed into the new religion.

Unsullied human mother of Christ—the warm human connection to God. (M)

Interesting concession to the human nurturing need not covered elsewhere in the system.

I was very devoted to her up until ten years ago when I started to look at the Church more closely. (F)

Have put her on hold.

She was conceived without Original Sin—the Immaculate Conception—so that she'd be the appropriate vessel of God's son. Impregnated by God through the Holy Ghost. Bailed out by Joseph. Carried bodily to heaven at her death. I bought this too. (F)

An attempt to incorporate pagan earth/mother/goddess beliefs into a new religion to attract followers.

Nice lady. (M).

Presented in a much too passive way.

The mother of Jesus, chosen because of her virtue. (F)

Haven't thought of her a lot lately. Sometimes I wonder what she was really like. She always came across so anti-septic.

Pure and holy, the perfect woman to emulate. (F)

I think her image was created by men as a means of controlling women. I like to think of her as having had a great sex life!

Girls and Sexuality

The Virgin birth teaching led inevitably to the conclusion that Catholic girls should also be pure. We got the message, by the time we were 10 or 11, that purity was good and that we were to guard against "impure thoughts and desires", meaning that we were to fight *normal* sexual thoughts and feelings. We were also taught that sex before marriage was a sin; it was implied that sex *after* marriage was not the best, either. Nuns and priests were somehow better people because they didn't have sex and were therefore closer to Christ. The difficulty, of course, is that we were ordinary girls with normal sexual curiosity. This curiosity was regarded as sinful, a fact which created untold amounts of sexual guilt. For those unlucky girls who were discovered in sexual play, additional shame was in store. Even very young children felt "wrong" or "bad" for having sexual thoughts or engaging in sexual play. Below are some examples of messages received in childhood by respondents to the survey. The question posed was: "What did the Church teach you about sex?"

"Dirty. Don't enjoy it."

"Don't talk about it or do it."

"It's bad."

"Nothing! It's negative, denied, a sin."

"It's dark and private, and tolerated for procreation only."

"It's not discussed; it's only for having children, a no-no otherwise."

"Sex is a sin!"

"Wasn't discussed, or if it was, it was wrong."

"Nothing was ever mentioned except purity."

"An evil part of one's person that has limited use: for procreation in marriage."

"The part of ourselves that is not connected at all to the rest of our bodies. It's just for creating children."

Most Catholic girls (and many Catholic boys) remained virgins until marriage, particularly those raised in the first half of this century. The mixed message inherent in teachings regarding sexuality became clearer at the time of marriage, when sexuality was then permitted, *for the purpose of procreation only*. Nowhere was it said that our bodies were to be enjoyed, to be cherished, to be used as a way to express joy, love and pleasure. Those who were Catholic when they married came to their husbands not only "pure" physically, but mentally and emotionally ill-equipped to deal with intimacy. If they had not learned how to have loving thoughts towards their own body, how could they be expected to give *and receive* love within their marriage? After all, Catholic girls were raised to emulate the Virgin Mary! Sexuality for procreation was allowed, but the message seemed to be to keep the chastity belt on at the same time, through carefully following the Church's edicts regarding masturbation, oral sex and birth control. Sex was allowed but you mustn't have too much fun. Following the rules closely seemed to guarantee this, as one survey responder explains:

"I realized I didn't believe a good portion of what the Church wanted me to believe, for example, in relation to sex. I think about my boyfriend (who later became my husband) and sex before marriage. I knew it wasn't the thing to do and I thought 'was it wrong because there wasn't a commitment there, (which was important to me), or because the *Church* said it was wrong?' Once my husband and I were engaged it seemed okay, yet in the eyes of the Church it *wasn't* okay. I felt really confused in my head. Later, when we were meeting with the priest who was going to marry us, he said that he wouldn't marry us unless we were going into the marriage planning to have children. I thought 'What business is it of yours? Are you going to help raise these children?' The whole issue raised a lot of conflict (even though we *were* planning to have children) because—here sits this man in front of us who has never had a family of his own telling us he wouldn't marry us, even though we love each other and plan to be together, because of *children*. Has he ever raised children and gone through the hardships of that, or wondered if he'd have enough money to support them and feed them and care for them properly, much less wondered if he had the personality that could provide a nurturing environment for a child? It just didn't make sense."

Some recovering Catholics also had positive experiences intermingled with the others, which may at times have added to the confusion:

"I attended a few retreats and organized youth events during my early adolescence. Those were usually very positive. One in particular I remember as being quite helpful at the time. The organizers dealt with the issue of sex during this retreat. They showed a fairly complete film, as I remember, describing sexual intercourse between a man and a woman in biological detail. I don't believe there was any heavy moral messages given, except that sex was something that was better to wait until marriage for. At the same time, I spent the better part of my 20's struggling with my sexuality in relation to certain aspects of my religious upbringing. As I filtered out the messages I received as a child and young adult that were manipulations rather than something I could actually use, I came to peace with a lot of my feelings. My biggest problems always stemmed from what I was taught and what I perceived as reality."

When asked about what they were taught regarding masturbation, most former Catholic girls said they had no knowledge of the word until they were older:

"In college another Catholic girl told me that she masturbated and that it was a lot of fun. *Fun?!* I remember acting cool but inside feeling incredibly fearful. I don't think, although this is amazing to say, that I had ever touched my genitals except to wash myself. I was *very* afraid of them and what they stood for... sin, basically. I didn't sit around thinking about it but I didn't touch them, either! After that I started to masturbate but at times I still feel guilty and have to work with myself about it even though I'm now in my 40's."

Another woman had this to say:

"Masturbation was never addressed *ever*. I didn't even know what it was until I came across the word when I was 14 years old, flipping through a book for teens. Even then, they didn't really say what it was. I had to do some research to find out exactly what it meant, and then I realized I'd been doing this nameless thing for quite a while. Did I feel guilty about it in relation to my upbringing? Yes, especially at first, but not because of something specifically ever said to me. It just felt like something must be wrong. The fantasies I had also caused me lots of guilty feelings. When I was about 16 years old I read a letter to an advice columnist from a young woman who was dating a boy who she really liked and felt she might end up having sex with. This was something she didn't want to do until she was married, but in the meantime she didn't know what to do about her strong feelings. The columnist suggested masturbating before she went out with him as a way of dealing with that. I began to see masturbation as a positive thing. By the time I was 18 years old I had few guilty feelings about the act. It is an issue that I see our culture not dealing with very well. I had a conversation recently with a male friend of mine, also Catholic, who was complaining about the heavy guilt trip he got about masturbation as a boy, that he didn't see girls getting. Also that it was something that boys had little control over. Personally, I don't think that girls necessarily have less of a sex drive at that age. The fact that it is something not acknowledged by adults or peers creates an atmosphere of isolation around an individual's feelings: that individual not knowing whether any other girl her age is experiencing the same thing. An unspoken taboo, so to speak."

As the above writer suggests, sexual difficulties and confusion were certainly not limited to girls, but the process was somewhat different for boys.

BOYS AND THEIR BODIES

Boys also received instructions to remain pure; however these messages seem to have been delivered in a more direct way. Boys were instructed by their Catholic parents, or by priests in grade school or C.C.D. classes, not to touch their genitals except for cleanliness, and they were discouraged from masturbation with the admonition that it was a mortal sin. (As already mentioned, it never occurred to many Catholic girls that masturbation was even an option). Regardless of behavior, intense guilt and anxiety for both sexes seems to have been steadily present for many Catholics, throughout childhood and often into adulthood. The fact that the Gospels totally ignore the issue of Jesus' sexuality (and other aspects of his manhood) made the sexual feelings of Catholic boys appear glaringly sordid by contrast. The Church used this contrast as an opportunity to remind us of our "shame." Jesus' father Joseph comes across as an asexual, nondescript character. In almost every picture ever painted he is seen wearing brown clothing, standing in the background, with Mary, Jesus, and even animals metaphorically occupying a more significant role.

Jesus, Joseph, the male clergy, and numerous unmarried male saints were depicted as role models for Catholic boys. None of these men were shown to have rich, vibrant relationships with women that included a natural human expression of their sexuality. We were taught that Jesus was a man "just like us", and yet the Church and therefore, its people, have had a hard time allowing that to be true. Catholic boys, taught to repress their sexuality, were instructed to venerate the Virgin Mary, and align themselves in Spirit (though not in body) with Catholic girls, whose devotion to the Virgin Mary and "purity" encouraged similar repression. Many of the male survey respondents said they had little understanding of how to relate to girls or women in a straightforward way, having been encouraged to avoid actual relationships with the opposite sex. Tim talks about his experience:

"I went to a seminary high school and when I graduated I was approaching college and women in the way a grade school kid would. There were a lot of things I wasn't comfortable with, like asking a woman for a date or trying to start a sexual relationship. Women were a non-issue in the seminary. They didn't actually come out and say that women were evil or anything like that but sex was not for outside of wedlock, and for us (seminary students) sex was a sin, taboo. There was never an approach, a teaching about any of it. They didn't approach the idea of normal sexual sensations or sexual dreams but the impression I got was that when you did masturbate or had bad thoughts you dealt with it through the Confessional. The idea was that you do the best you can with these issues. We were all evil to begin with, we knew, and you just have to work to get better. You didn't talk to anybody about it because everybody was in the same situation in terms of brainwashing so you weren't ever going to admit to someone you masturbated. That would be a sign you were weak. I *did* masturbate but I also felt weak and less than up to par. There was some homosexuality that went on among the boys at my boarding school which I think is related."

Tim's experience was representative of a seminary high school setting, distinctive in that it was preparing him to take on the life of a priest. As preparation for going out to counsel and support members of parishes, these boys were often sadly uninformed about women and their sexual and emotional needs. It is not surprising that married couples, intent on developing intimacy in their relationship, have often received little substantial help from priests and nuns.

Tim's experience in a seminary school may seem idiosyncratic and unrepresentative of most Catholic boys. Jim talked about what *he* was taught in his Catholic grade school about sexuality:

"The priest would come in a couple of times a week to my school and give a Catechism lesson. The priests were the official purveyors of the dogma but the nuns were active, too. The session might be on the 8th Commandment, Thou Shalt not Commit Adultery. The priest might say 'What does adultery mean?' Maybe somebody knew. 'Now this doesn't have to do with you children but some things do have to do with you children', and then he'd list them. 'You can't play with yourself, your private parts.' And there were code words: self-pollution, self-abuse. It was clear they meant masturbation or taking pleasure in your body. You could touch yourself to wash or urinate but once you took pleasure in yourself that was a sin and that sent you to Hell unless you went to Confession."

This type of training before puberty was a preparation for adolescence, when boys typically undergo intense physical changes resulting in heightened sexual awareness. What happened to teenage boys who were taught that sexual thoughts were unacceptable? Jim was asked what happened in puberty:

"Incredible stress! It was awful, so painful because I was a normal child with a normal body. I pushed the desires down, and of course, they came bursting up. I kept going to Confession. In Confession I'd have to say I abused myself 20 times, 30 times that week, and it was terribly shaming."

And Helen:

"I was sexually very repressed and was told by my Catholic mother that sex was something I would be instructed about by my husband. I thought at age 14 that you could get pregnant from kissing. The effect was that I remained a virgin because of fear of getting pregnant. When my virginity became too great a burden to bear, I found a guy who had had a vasectomy. This was his only redeeming quality. Shortly after that I met my husband. I'm surprisingly open-minded and comfortable about sex, and uninhibited about the whole thing, given my background; however I am also a non-joiner, non-conformist, and overall rebel, which may account for some of it, particularly as I have the opinion that the Catholic attitude about sex is all about a primal fear of the power of women's bodies, and a fear of a loss of control on the part of the male hierarchy."

And so many of us grew up and got married or began other significant relationships without the benefit of really useful information about sex. Sexuality was for procreative purposes only. This was taken very seriously by the Church. If a husband, for example, needed to give a sperm sample for medical reasons, he would have been instructed to ejaculate into his wife's vagina first, so as not to interfere with procreation, and then to collect it for medical reasons. The Church put many rules into effect which controlled minute aspects of couples' love lives, and which interfered with the creation of their own satisfying patterns of expression. In many cases, the Church's rules, supposedly instituted to protect the life process of unconceived and unborn children, effectively managed to undermine and disregard this life process, as well as the emotional and sexual health of the live adults in many Catholic bedrooms. Some couples managed to go on to have rich love lives, and yet my experience is that the specter of guilt continues to play itself out in one form or another, even to the present day.

John, a former Catholic who is divorced, had this to say about his sexual attitudes and how they have affected his adult life:

"Sex and sexual relationships were another study in conflict and confusion that continues to plague me to this day. Priests would tell us that sex was a beautiful thing only between married couples for the purpose of procreation. Well, if sex was such a beautiful thing, why did nuns and priests become celibate? In my mind, as a child, this was part of what sets them 'above' the rest of us. The birth of Jesus wasn't tainted by sex. Sex was something vaguely shameful, not to take pleasure in. But sex feels good! So you wind up sinning in having sex. I remember few incidences in my life where sex has not been accompanied by at least some small measure of guilt. So, here I am as an adult trying to have a healthy sex life while

feeling ashamed of my body and guilty about both the pleasure and the non-procreative nature of my endeavor."

If intentional non-procreative sex was taboo for married
couples, what was the teaching regarding homosexuality? Needless to say, it was considered a sin, and homosexual acts required
the sinner to go to Confession with an intention to change his or
her ways. For some former Catholics, particularly those who have
left the Church in recent days, this issue contributed greatly to
their decision to leave. One recovering Catholic said this:

> "I read a Pastoral letter that said the Church would accept
> homosexuals but said that what they *do* is wrong. I just can't
> see that. What they do may not be right for *us* but that doesn't
> mean it's not right for *them*. We have homosexual friends
> and I could never see taking the stance, in public or in the
> confines of my own mind, that what they do is wrong be-
> cause they're *people*, with their own issues and strengths. It
> isn't my choice, but if it makes them happy and helps them
> to grow, who's to say 'this is wrong'? I decided I didn't want
> to be part of a Church that made those kind of personal de-
> cisions for people. I wanted to be part of an organization that
> valued peoples' *own* powers of decision-making."

Whether younger or older, many of us were raised with a set of
rigid, guilt-producing, and repressive beliefs. At the very least we
entered adulthood with a certain amount of guilt and confusion
about our bodies. The adult part of ourselves may now think that
sexuality is great and that pleasure and rich, joyful lovemaking are
cornerstones of a good relationship. Why, then, do we often
struggle with our sexuality, and why has sexuality been particularly difficult for some of us over the years? No doubt there are a
number of cultural, historical, and societal reasons for problems
with sexuality. As Catholics, however, we learned the formula of

sex = sin = punishment. So, while the adult part of ourselves may be open and interested in sex, the child/teenager within us may continue to hold to the old beliefs and fears by setting up conflicts that incapacitate us from improving our love lives. If we heard as children that sex is for procreation only, how can we expect ourselves to love our own bodies, and our partner's body, and enjoy lovemaking for its own sake? To say that sex is for procreation only is to deny our humanity. We *do* have bodies, and our bodies are an obvious way of sharing and receiving love.

Few of us moved into adulthood without a good dose of guilt and confusion regarding sexuality. In Chapter 8 we will look at a variety of ways of working to change our perceptions of the body and sexuality, so as to move beyond rigid and confining rules which may still be affecting our present lives. The following chapter deals with the ways in which the body was connected, more specifically, with suffering and shame.

CHAPTER FOUR

SUFFERING AND SHAME

*S*uffering is assumed to be a powerful component of human experience, and is often described as an undesirable, but unavoidable part of human life. The Adult Children of Alcoholics movement (A.C.O.A.) and other self-help groups talk a lot about suffering in their meetings. In childhood, these individuals were often denied their feelings: of anger, fear, sadness, joy, and love. They are now learning to get back in touch with feelings and to allow them full expression. For many of us, as for them, the denial of feelings led to a tendency to see ourselves as victims, as martyrs. If our home life was not happy, taking the role of martyr came easily, for this role was encouraged by the Church. In looking back at our Catholic roots, the concepts of victim and sacrifice are familiar. Here is the definition of sacrifice from the 1950 version of the Boston Catechism:

"A sacrifice is the offering of a victim by a priest to God alone, and the destruction of it in some way to acknowledge that He is the Creator of all things. A gift offered to God in sacrifice we call a VICTIM. The perfect sacrifice was that of Christ on the Cross. The priest was the Son of God made man. He was also the VICTIM, since the gift was Himself, His own Precious Blood. He gave it to his Father to show Him His love and devotion. The Father was most pleased. He accepted the gift His Son offered Him and showed it by raising Him from the dead on Easter and bringing Him to heaven forty days later, on Ascension Day."

This encapsulates the teachings we received regarding the Crucifixion, sacrifice, suffering, and death. Many of us learned to accept these teachings as truth. The main messages we received as children were these:

1) Christ's suffering and death were meaningful gifts from Christ to God (implying that God thought the body was the best possible offering).
2) God needed us to "pay up" for our errors (ie. we *owe* him).
3) God felt that things were "even" after Christ's sacrifice (implying He had kept tabs on us, and then felt vindicated after the Crucifixion).
4) Pain and suffering are satisfying sacrifices for God. (God likes to see us suffer).
5) The main point of the Crucifixion is Christ's suffering.
6) The role of victim or martyr is desirable and should be emulated.

As a child, I remember thinking that it didn't make sense for God to have kept score of all our sins, or to have needed Christ as a sacrifice. I decided I must be wrong to think in this way, and these thoughts were immediately suppressed as I became more and more immersed in the rituals that reinforced the traditional Christian view. The phrase "Christ died for our sins" was set in stone. Much emphasis was put on the effects of Christ's suffering. The back cover of the Baltimore Catechism put it this way: "Think—how much Our Lord must have loved me to suffer those nails, those thorns, those bleeding wounds, such humilities, such heartbreak. Think about this for at least a minute every day." It is not surprising, in the face of this type of message, that love and pain became intertwined for many of us.

Most of our churches contained a large crucifix behind the altar which was very lifelike, with bloodied thorns and nails in Christ's feet and hands. This image was compelling. Several survey respondents said they could easily go into a trance-like state during Mass, imagining the pain and horror of Christ's Crucifixion. Feelings of loneliness and isolation seem typically to have accompanied this state of mind. In Catholic school and C.C.D. children were encouraged to contemplate the idea of Christ's sacrifice to God and to think about their need to be grateful to Christ. Strong, persuasive and emotionally evocative language was used to enhance the meaning of the Crucifixion. In addition, children were encouraged, throughout Lent and at other times, to make sacrifices the way Christ did, and to "offer up" their suffering to God. In this way, the whole concept of suffering took on a life of its own. Children read 'The Lives of the Saints' and felt the urge to identify with Saints who suffered severely. One survey respondent remembers tying up her feet tightly until they hurt and feeling "deliciously" martyred, while emulating her favorite saint. Another remembers feelings of frustration:

"When I suffered, I knew I had to offer it up to God. If you really got into it, suffering felt like an identity, but that had a problem, too. If I took pleasure in my suffering I felt ashamed, as though I was no longer giving God anything anymore because it was too much fun. I felt like I couldn't win! I also hated the idea that what I did have to offer was small, insignificant, and unworthy of God. Why bother?!

"If we did anything bad in Catholic grade school we were made to kneel on our hands in the hallway and told to offer it up. We made the Stations of the Cross on our knees. That was really painful. That was atonement—hurting yourself. I remember this story of a female saint who was beautiful, and she made herself ugly—she hurt her face—and that bothered me. She was born beautiful and somehow that was bad and this was saintly, to destroy your beauty. These saints, they sometimes didn't even wait for someone else to torture them, they just went out and did it to themselves."

As small children, eager to learn and ready to please, many of us lived with feelings of guilt and fear. After all, it was our sin that made it necessary for Christ to die in this horrible way. *We killed Him.* If this sounds overly dramatic, consider this prayer for children taken from a pamphlet from the 1940's:

"Dear Jesus, I want to cry, too. I am so sorry that You, who love Me, are suffering so much. I know You are my dear Brother, and You are dying for my sake. Forgive me for my sins. I am sorry they are causing Your death. My sins have made my parents unhappy, too. They made my companions sin. Dear Jesus, I hate my sins. Please don't ever let me sin again."

Like the soldiers at the foot of the Cross, we were responsible for his death. It was on our heads: a pretty heavy responsibility for a 5 year-old, don't you think? In addition, we were constantly reminded of this: in Church, at school, at home, and every time we saw a crucifix. We subsequently discovered that one way of dealing with this guilt was to identify with Christ—to have sufferings, aches, and pains of our own. This made us feel more like Christ, less like the murderers we knew we were, and it was sanctioned and encouraged by the Church itself.

The next step was to "offer it up", as a way of getting God to witness the fact that we were going through our suffering for *Him*. It was a way of letting go of the guilt in exchange for inflicting pain onto ourselves. For those of us who attended Catholic grade schools, the nuns often acted as "soldiers at the foot of Christ", using a ruler instead of a lance to remind us of our "unworthiness". Needless to say, this institutionalized sado-masochism had profound and lasting effects.

Through this pattern of guilt, suffering and pain, many of us have learned to play the role of victim, to a greater or lesser extent, depending on a variety of factors: our personalities, the decade in which we were raised, the emotional climate of our homes. Had we been able to acknowledge our natural human feelings of anger (a capital sin, in the eyes of the Church), we could have saved ourselves untold amounts of confusion, frustration, and guilt.

The role of "victim" also put many of us, and many of our parents, in a position of separation—separation from ourselves, separation from a spouse or children, and separation from the world. While it is certainly true that millions of people throughout the world understand this feeling of separation, the emotional "aura" of our Catholic training was specific and clearly defined. Going back into Catholic issues to unravel our experience is simply a way of acknowledging our roots. One interviewee offered these thoughts on the subject of suffering:

> "Suffering is good; pride is a sin; silence is a virtue; it's better to give than to receive; vanity is a sin; these were all part of my religious upbringing. My mother was a strong advocate of suffering and silence. Actually, I feel that there is usefulness to all these things, it's just that they're taken to such an extreme. A certain amount of suffering is okay, but not knowing how to ask for help, something I continue to have a huge block about, can be detrimental. Too much pride

will definitely get a person in trouble, but feeling good about yourself and what you do in this life is great for self-esteem. Giving is wonderful, but receiving can be another form of giving. If you've ever tried to give something to someone who refuses to receive, you'll know what I mean. I do have a hard time saying no, saying what I want, enjoying myself too much or for too long, being the center of attention, feeling okay about not being virginal. Actually, the more I think about it, the more I see it in my life. I practically draw a blank at times when someone asks me what I want. My usual response is 'Well, whatever *you* want,' whether it's concerning the kind of pizza we're getting, sex, how my work station is set up. Sometimes I wonder whether I even know what I want, but on further introspection, I realize that it's more of a matter of expectation. When my expectations are low, I'm not disappointed. I don't feel worthy enough to expect things. These aren't huge problems in my life, but I see them infiltrating in small ways, here and there, all over the place, and sometimes I'm amazed at how incapacitated I will become over some things. I have found myself a few times unable to speak, when asked if I'd like to make love to my husband, and I've wanted to say 'no'. I don't want to blame this completely on my religious upbringing. I know they have been reinforced by other things. The connection is hard to deny, though."

The theme of forgiveness permeated Catholic teachings, of course, but the mixed messages dominated the scene. "Remember that Christ died for you" encouraged some of us to feel guilt, while forgiveness messages encouraged us to release others *from* guilt. The fact that both messages were given simultaneously confused the issue. None of the respondents to the questionnaire remember being encouraged to forgive *themselves* for their own mistakes. All said they had been told to ask God's forgiveness, but none really *felt* forgiven.

Can we really accept the notion that God is some sort of vampire who was out for blood, and who believed that Christ's death would be the ideal gift? It was as though Christ's "perfect sacrifice" brought him into a wonderful position with God while the rest of us on earth continued to goof up. As 7 or 8 year-olds the guilt impact of still being "bad" (even though Christ went to all that trouble) was ongoing and pervasive. This was often enhanced by the criticism and severity of some of the clergy, who were themselves controlled by these same feelings of guilt.

The emphasis on suffering, torture and pain certainly existed before Christianity, and is a reminder of the pagan emphasis on blood sacrifice. Unnatural events, such as floods or famine, were then viewed as punishments from the gods, indicating that serious sins had been committed. The gods needed to be appeased at all costs, and blood sacrifice was used for this purpose. The belief that Christ died to appease an angry God, who kept a running tab of our sins, seems a pagan notion to many recovering Catholics, and no longer believable as a means of understanding oneself in relation to others or to God. Many former Catholics who are also no longer Christian are experimenting with other means of acknowledging these essential connections.

When questioned about their childhood impressions of the Redemption and their current views, survey respondents provided the following:

PAST	PRESENT
Jesus died because I'm a bad person. I felt shame.	A great guilt trip even better than human sacrifice. You get to sacrifice God!

Christ redeemed us from our sinfulness. Now we *can* go to heaven *if*... I felt very guilty.	An arbitrary, unnecessary doctrine. Follows from the belief that we are inherently evil.
Christ died for me and I should be grateful.	This brings back old tapes that I was bad. I don't believe it.
Redemption: another word that always scared me—"died for my sins!" I tried to be so good. I always felt fear.	Redemption? Still hate that word!
Even then, I couldn't find any part of me that needed redeeming.	I'm not willing to change who I am to accommodate beliefs that don't fit for me.
Jesus died to make up for our original sin (as committed by Adam).	Irrelevant in reality but a potentially useful psychological exercise to overcome guilt for those who can believe it.
I should be grateful for Christ's dying.	I don't like to discuss this.

In adulthood, many of us live with underlying, day to day feelings of fear or anxiety, seeing ourselves as guilty and deserving of punishment. We now administer this punishment to ourselves directly. For example, we might unwittingly organize friends and family to punish us, to one degree or another, as we move into a cycle of anger, guilt, fear, and punishment. During our childhood we had no control over what we were taught. In contrast, we now have the capacity to look at events (including the Crucifixion) in ways which feel life-enhancing, self-supporting, and positive. Although this may be happening in some churches in the present, the long-standing focus on sacrifice, suffering, and death remains a powerful symbol of limitation, lack, and inadequacy, both in ourselves and in others. Even those of us who no longer hold this view, or who see God as quintessentially loving, find ourselves playing the victim, from the moment we wake up ("Yuck! It's raining outside", "it's Monday", "it's Winter") to the time we go to bed ("What a day", "I'm so glad it's over", "I'm so stressed"). It is also important to note that the severity of the event is not necessarily proportional to the *degree* of suffering. I myself am quite capable of experiencing suffering while doing two loads of wash, feeling victimized because my family won't sort out dirty clothes from clean ones, thinking they don't love me and are looking for ways to punish me. This may sound unnecessarily dramatic, but it is nonetheless true. We're often simply not *consciously aware* of our underlying feelings of worthlessness, and are more content to settle an issue by blaming others or going into a funk, both postures coming from a victimized stance, and both speaking to our need for punishment.

One recovering Catholic explained her feelings in this way:

"My Catholic mother was a great sufferer. Come to think of it, most of the Catholic mothers I knew were great sufferers, but came from different ethnic backgrounds. The Irish mothers gnashed their teeth pretty well, but so did the Italian mothers. I've heard people say that strong demonstration of feeling is *strictly* cultural, but I think it's related to the Catholic thing. The Virgin Mary at the foot of the Cross seemed the prototype for suffering. Between the nuns, the Virgin Mary and my mother—who made emotional and physical suffering an art form—I learned how to suffer well. I am still working on changing this. Don't tell me that Prot-

69

estants suffer in the same way, because my observations are that they don't put much stock in suffering. Maybe that is why, as a child, I used to see Protestants as very bland and boring. Maybe they just don't have a suffering addiction the way us Catholics do!"

When asked to give her childhood definition of God, another respondent wrote the following: "God is our heavenly Father and Creator who loves us and wants the best for us, but has to punish us when we're bad." The problem for little children who learned this (and the adults who have supported it for so many generations) is that we keep being bad, in one way or another, for all of our lives, and so we never move beyond the childish merry-go-round of naughtiness and punishment.

We mustn't doubt for one minute that some members of the Church's hierarchy, at various times in history and through various means, saved lives and kept families and communities intact and functioning by this teaching that God is capable of being punitive. For many of the people interviewed, however, this issue alone resulted in their decision to leave the Church. Many of these individuals had felt controlled by the Church, and were clearly aware of the expectation to think, act, and speak only in ways sanctioned by the Church. When the beliefs of the individual contradicted its teachings, the Church, acting as the voice of God, chastised the individual, using guilt as a primary tool to pressure him or her to re-evaluate their thinking and return to the right course.

For those of us who left the Church, unable to accept some of its standards beliefs, the use of guilt as a controlling strategy no longer worked—or so we thought. We found it harder and harder to accept the Church as our spiritual "parent". Many of us also found it hard to accept the role of *God* as "parent". What we were really letting go of here was the intellectual notion of God as a *critical* parent, whose primary focus is to root out evil, using punishment as the main deterrent. The problem, again, is that despite having written off concepts of sin, punishment and suffering inherent in our background, our inner child goes along unhappily seeking and receiving punishment, and believing in her own innate badness, thereby preserving and repeating the self-defeating patterns of our childhood:

> "If it wasn't my Catholic parents berating me, it was a Catholic nun. I spent a lot of my adult life apologizing for everything, to everyone. I don't do that anymore but, boy, I can still shame myself on the *inside*."

So we find that we are in a dilemma: we earnestly and sensibly wish to avoid punishment, but find it impossible to escape being *bad*, on a fairly frequent basis (for example, we are impatient with our kids, or are too controlling with our colleagues). At best we are one step ahead of guilt, and at worst we are being immobilized by it; in either case, an inordinate amount of emotional and psychological energy is being used up in fending off punishment—or death—leaving precious little time for actually celebrating our alive-ness. In this way, the Crucifixion keeps happening, day after day, week after week, year after year, encouraged by our persistence in seeing ourselves in black and white. The only way of being truly reconciled to ourselves is through accepting that we are human, that we are learning, and that we need to feel extraordinary compassion for ourselves. Intellectually, this might be easy to grasp; it's the kind of thing we read and have heard in many places (even in church, sometimes). The real challenge is to convey these understandings to our inner child, who doesn't buy it and is hell-bent on looking for new and improved opportunities for Self-Crucifixion.

Recently, in a group session, a member who is a recovering Catholic announced, in a somewhat guilty yet angry manner, that he no longer wanted to attend the group, that he was feeling the need in group to "keep the sword ready" to defend himself from the rest of us, because he shared a different view on a particular issue. I think he was prepared to be punished by us for leaving. The group decided to put aside its own swords and hurts (in the form of feeling rejected and manipulated) and refused to punish him. Instead, we asked him what would feel good as a way of supporting him. He asked to be held, which surprised all of us. We did as he asked, while he cried buckets of tears, not only tears of sadness for years of pain in childhood, but tears of amazed joy that we responded to his anger with love.

It is incredible to acknowledge that, like vampires, we are very comfortable with the darkness of our own pain, anger, sin, worry, and fear, which we hold onto like a teddy bear, but then are paralyzed by light. Just try letting yourself off the hook for a simple infraction. Many of the respondents indicated they were unable to do this, not only for more "serious" mistakes, but for such trivial mistakes as getting to the grocery store and forgetting they had forgotten the shopping list! This is not to say we need to abolish guilt; the trick is to simply become aware that what we're doing isn't working. This takes it completely out of the realm of good and bad. The polarities of good and bad make us uncomfortable, regardless of which extreme is involved. If we decide that both ourselves and our actions are "bad", then we need punishment. If we decide our actions are "good", we still feel "bad" because we know we're capable of screwing up again at any time, even though we're "good" at the moment. Simply stating that something is *working* makes more sense, and most importantly, gives us an energy break, because we don't need to go through the usual anger/guilt/suffering routine. Self-punishment also stops us from connecting with other people, not only because we're low-energy, but because our guilt tells us we're unacceptable. We go out into the world in this state, making little eye contact (to avoid getting the punishment we think we deserve), and have trouble giving of ourselves, having been taught to see ourselves as unworthy.

Seeing our thoughts and actions as generally "working" or generally "not working"—as opposed to "good" or "bad"—has a second, potentially powerful effect: it allows these thoughts and actions freedom of movement. We don't get clogged up with the kind of limited thinking that impairs our creativity. We're able to detach from the part of ourselves that wants to drag us down before it hangs us on the Cross. This is the part we have trouble seeing as *inside* of ourselves, and which the Church referred to as "the Devil". In some ways it felt safer to see this tendency as existing outside of ourselves. The problem is that it also didn't allow us to feel a sense of control, of mastery, over our own lives. Recognition of our human capacity to create messes in our lives, without seeing ourselves as faulty at the core, is freeing. Again, if we're not constantly combatting feelings of shame, we have the energy, creativity, and mental clarity to learn from our experience. It allows daily life to become an experimental workshop or laboratory. In a science lab, researchers don't beat themselves up when an experiment fails, because the work is just that, an experiment, and because it is simply part of the job. Instead they recognize that their mistakes are important, necessary and useful tools, which actually contribute to new discoveries and solutions to problems.

How were we able to survive, emotionally and spiritually, in this spirit of suffering and punishment? How were we able to tolerate the restrictions, the penances, the sacrifices, and the shame this entailed? One explanation might be that our Catholic teachings, in their black and white way, offered heaven as a reward for our trials. For many of us, and for our parents, life (black) would be supplanted by the perfect life to come (white). The idea that much of our daily suffering might be due to our own negative thinking and restriction of spirit, did not occur to us. While patiently tolerating our suffering here on earth, we were told to think about heaven and all that would eventually await us. The next chapter will look more closely at our beliefs about salvation, and their effects in our past and present lives.

CHAPTER FIVE

SALVATION

A s Catholics, we were strongly motivated by the desire to "get to heaven". Heaven was described to us as a wonderful place, full of joy, and with no suffering or unhappiness to mar its magnificence. Our every need and desire fulfilled, we would be free to enjoy God's love for all of eternity. At the same time, we were instructed that heaven came with a price tag. We had to earn our way there through positive actions on earth. Just as we put money into our savings account each week, we needed to make spiritual "deposits" so that we could afford to go to heaven. Different types of indulgences or special prayers, if said properly and with devotion, would enable us to spend less time in Purgatory. It is humorous in looking back to note that conventional earth time was used to figure the details: for example, we would receive 300 or 500 days less of Purgatory time if we said the right prayers. A group of men sat round a table, one can assume, and actually decided how much credit God would give; and they did it using earth time, to boot!

We were taught that Purgatory was a necessary "waiting station" where we would be purified. Purgatory was not a trip to the Bahamas. A pamphlet entitled 'The Savior's Fountains', written in 1944, described it this way:

> "The punishment of Purgatory, like that of Hell, is twofold, the pain of loss and the pain of sense. The former is by far the greater: one glimpse of God and then banishment from His sight. St. Catherine tells us that the suffering soul is entirely resigned to the will of its Creator. It loves its very pains and rejoices in them because they are a holy ordinance of God. Apart from their intense pain and horrible suffering, the most pathetic thing about the Poor Souls is their utter helplessness. Purgatory, then, is a state of excruciating pain and torment. All of us may expect through God's mercy to experience a painful sojourn in this prison of God's love. How long will we be compelled to languish there? That depends on the number of unpardonable venial sins and the amount of punishment still due at the time of death for sins forgiven but not satisfied for."

This passage is an excellent example of the Church's invitation to its people to engage in exquisite sado-masochistic fantasies and expectations for the next world, which many, as we have already seen, successfully demonstrated in this world as well. Again, we have the vision of an Unsatisfied, Angry God, who is obsessed with being paid back for the mistakes we made on earth. At the same time we were told that God's mercy allowed us to experience the privilege of this painful experience. A survey respondent had this to say:

> "We were made to go to Confession weekly before Mass. They told us we should be Perfect but they clearly *expected* us to be sinners! Purgatory and hell were waiting for us.

They expected, and we also expected, that we would do time in Purgatory. No way out. Was the God that set up this system going to let me off the hook? Look what his perfect son went through! I remember, even as a child, wondering what kind of a God is it that creates mankind then sets him up to fail. Right from the start with the Tree of Knowledge in the Garden of Eden down to eternal damnation and Purgatory. This seemed incongruous with the image of an all-loving father."

Here is another example:

"I knew from my education that the majority of mankind was not going to make it into heaven. This just didn't seem fair to me. Thinking about this God terrified me. On the other hand, thinking it didn't seem fair *also* terrified me. How dare I think bad thoughts about God? What would my punishment be for that? What could I tell the priest?"

Often, saints and other holy people were said to possess special information regarding the afterlife, and their experiences were enshrined by the Church as a means of controlling earthly behavior. One priest wrote the following in one of his pamphlets:

"If we look into the revelations of Sister Frances of Pompelona we shall find among some hundreds of cases that by far the greater majority suffered 30, 40, or 60 years. As to the seeming length of time from the extremity of pain, there are many instances of souls appearing an hour or two after death and thinking they had been many years in Purgatory."

Like the boogie-man in the closet, this type of pronouncement was effective in controlling those young souls who depended on the Church for their sense of identity. Perhaps the need to be scared by our own shadows is universal; it has certainly been true for many of us raised Catholic. I have noticed that people who converted to Catholicism tended, even in former days, to disbelieve these types of ideas. This also seems to hold true for Catholics who had one parent of another faith, and for those whose parents went to public schools or were discouraged from this type of thinking by their parents.

The tendency to scare ourselves, learned in our young Catholic days, can be seen in our interpretations of many beliefs. Hell, Purgatory, the Crucifixion, the Last Judgment—all of these were frightening. Our efforts were never good enough and the message was given that if we didn't scare ourselves we would somehow lose sight of our inferiority. The following is from Christ within my Heart—Prayers Before and After Holy Communion:

> "Believing in You, I feel my nothingness. I know that I am a sinner. So often I have offended You. You have forgiven numerous offenses. Now I fall before You. May my lowliness and nothingness draw Your eyes towards me! Does not your heart go out to the lowly, and do not Your graces visit those who are conscious of their weaknesses? I am also aware that, if I have avoided evil or done good in the past, it was with Your cooperation.

> My unworthiness overwhelms me, and yet must I not feel that it is the very condition of Your coming to me? During Your days on earth You sought out sinners, and upon them showered tenderest mercies. Behold I am prostrate before You, weak, needy, hungry, in dire need of You. Come to me, O merciful and bountiful Lord."

If we did make it to heaven, we were taught that life would be eternally joyous, as we would be allowed to live with God forever. Heaven was not emphasized, however. Hell and Purgatory exercised the greatest degree of power in our imaginative life. The following are some comments by survey respondents. Those in the left column indicate what the respondents were taught as children regarding heaven. The comments on the right indicate their present day beliefs.

PAST	PRESENT
Heaven? It's way up there!	Heaven is under our feet as well as over our heads.
Heaven was very vague—eternal happiness.	Afterlife? I do believe in some state of existence for our "soul". Who knows what sort? I don't.
Where I would go some day if I was good.	Planes where souls go depending on karmas and if they have a Perfect Living Master.
The ideal place to be—eternal reward for being good. God, angels, "up in the clouds", sacrifice.	The carrot on the stick to motivate and control morals and social behavior.
Everyone went to heaven, but there were lots of loopholes.	The next life is an extension of this one.
Sounded like a boring place.	No comment.
A place of mystery and fantasy and being somewhere that was beautiful, and being with relatives who had died.	A place of love and peace.
Great, but who was good enough?	I think it's simply a change in states, a different level of existence.

How does the concept of Purgatory and heaven effect our present lives? Purgatory, in essence, is the teaching that *you can't have it all*. Those of us who were raised with this idea may be carrying it around with us into the present. We may be living lives imbued with limitations we have placed upon ourselves, with the assumption that true happiness, both on earth and in the hereafter, is simply not possible. If this is true, why bother?

A survey respondent provided his ideas:

"When I was young, I remember thinking a lot about limbo, as we called it then, and just how painful that would be—waiting for God, so to speak. I got the idea that I'd be stuck between heaven and hell—that I wouldn't actually be able to feel good, the way I would in heaven, and at the same time, it wouldn't be the torture that hell would be. I used to think it would be like having my leg stuck in a bear trap. I'd know that sooner or later someone would come and get me out but in the meantime, I'd be in pain. I think this was pretty much the idea the Church wanted me to get. The trouble was that I took it all in and took *myself* to Purgatory, beginning at age 10 or so probably. Why wait, avoid the rush! I think now that I was really scared of suddenly feeling all that pain when I died and I didn't know when that might be. If I started early, I'd be used to it. I feel sad to say that I have probably been in Purgatory my whole life".

If it is true that we are able to react to events in our lives in any number of ways, we have the choice of viewing work stress, a financial problem, an illness, or a death in a way that moves us forward, *or* in a way that keeps us "in limbo". We alone can decide how many days, months, or years we need to spend forgiving *ourselves* for taking wrong turns or being angry at the world for allowing painful things to happen. We don't need an angry, revengeful God any longer.

CHAPTER SIX

MEN AND WOMEN IN THE CHURCH

THE ROLE OF MEN

n American Catholic families, the discovery that a son had a vocation to the priesthood was a cause for celebration. Priests were seen as being "next to God". To become a father of children was acceptable, but to become a Father of the Church was undoubtedly an indication of special favor from God. In one edition of the Baltimore Catechism printed in the 1950's, a drawing depicted a couple being married on one side of the page. The other side showed a nun and a priest. The captions underneath the drawing of the married couple indicated this to be "good", while a religious vocation was described as "best". Priests were seen, by both adults and children, as special people, having superior spiritual skills and powers in the same way that doctors had superior medical powers. The whole ethos of the Mass, with its Vestments and incense and chalices, and ritual symbols: all contributed to this image. The priest wore clothing unlike ours, spoke Latin at Mass, and was seen as God's chosen representative. Most children and adults took the role of priest very seriously, emphasizing the special powers he possessed. If the adults occasionally saw Father Flynn having a few extra drinks at a party or cheating at golf, this was most likely dismissed or seen as endearing. For many decades the clergy and parishioners remained in denial about the fact that priests were real, live human beings, with ordinary needs, problems, worries and insecurities just like ours. This denial was a natural outgrowth of the teachings. Priests were representatives of Christ. We were encouraged to see Christ himself when attending Mass. The Church instructed us to follow the directives of our priest in all matters, knowing that Christ was essentially speaking through him.

Many priests have helped countless individuals, young and old, throughout this century and before. Acts of true love and appreciation have been fostered by priests in innumerable ways. The capacity to draw people together is a special skill. It is not, however, a skill which all clergy have. Many priests, born into families just like their parishioners, experienced physical, emotional or sexual abuse from their parents, and must as a result have been prone to feeling identity confusion and lack of clarity regarding their strengths and limitations; these traits were inevitably brought into their adult lives, and influenced their judgment and decision-making. The Church's command to pray, offer it up, fast, or do penance in the face of personal life problems could not have been any more sufficient for clergy than it was for parishioners, as an exclusive method for dealing with these life issues. Priests were no more immune than the rest of us to an underlying dislike of the self, nurtured during the early years; but priests may perhaps have had an even harder time with this, *because* they were supposed to be closer to God. Parishioners were expected to sin from time to time, while priests were supposed to be above all of that. Obviously, a priest and his superior would both know if serious problems arose, but great care was taken to ensure that lay people *didn't* know, for example, when a priest had had an affair. After all, we were all dependent on him. What would have happened if we discovered he had problems that needed help like the rest of us? The Church's fantasy may have been that the whole structure would come toppling down. The priest, after all, was the main expert on everything—spiritual issues, family life, marriage, and sexuality. If he acknowledged confusion and limitation, how could the rest of us survive?

Part of the underlying problem here seems to lie in the notion that the priest on the altar was not merely representing Christ—he *was* Christ. Many of the survey respondents indicated that they felt considerable anger as adults at the assumption that an "unmarried male virgin" (to quote one of them) could advise them in matters related to parenthood, sexuality, and relationships. This assumption *is* unreasonable and unfair to the priests themselves: they have been expected to be all and know all, and to have attained a level of wisdom about intimacy and human relationships in the face of little actual experience in this area. (Ironically, many *recovering* Catholics seem to be more able to see priests in this more humane and compassionate light than some of their practicing counterparts). The Catholic Church did not acknowledge its priests' masculinity, as related to sexuality and intimate relationships.

Some priests of recent years have opted to ignore the dictates of the Church with regard to sexual behavior, but this is still handled very secretively by the priest himself. Many former Catholics who have recently left the Church see this as unfortunate, for it deprives both the priest and the lay person of a richer, fuller understanding of love and sexuality as seen through the lens of spirituality. Seeing ordinary life experience as inferior to the life of the Spirit is demeaning to the beauty and potential in everyday life. The Church has needed its priests to remain pure, devoted, and Christ-like in order to protect the duality of the relationship between priest and lay person, with the priest taking the role of Christ (perfect and elevated), and the lay people taking the role of sinners (imperfect and ordinary).

All this seems particularly dysfunctional, bearing in mind the amount of outstanding litigation against Catholic priests for inappropriate sexual conduct, including sexual abuse of children, sexual advances to lay persons, voyeurism, and other illegal sexual behavior. Alcoholism among priests has also been a serious ongoing problem. Clearly, priests were and still are ordinary people, people who have personal problems, just like the rest of us.

Several survey respondents indicated that they could never return to the Church while it remains male dominated, and while the men themselves continued to be deprived of the full, ordinary, messy life of relationships and parenting that most of us experience. In the words of one interviewee who has only recently left the Church:

"I can't swallow the fact that all these priests are engaging in sexual misconduct, and still buy the Church's view that marriage and sexuality is somehow inferior to the celibate life. It seems so obvious to me that sexuality needs to be embraced in a healthy, accepting way, not only by lay persons, but by the clergy as well. And I think the Gospel authors were conflicted like everyone else, and just because they chose not to discuss Christ's sexuality, doesn't mean that he wasn't sexual or that he didn't think that loving sexuality was a great thing. Sexuality *will* be expressed. The way it is expressed is dictated by society's attitude about it. Seeing priests as sexless can result in inappropriate sexual behavior on their part. Seeing them as normal sexual beings can lead to normal, healthy sexual behavior."

This leads to the specific issue of priests' relationships with women. Again, the notion comes into play that the priest, on the altar, not only represents Christ but *is* Christ. Perhaps the difficulty in envisioning priests in a married state is related to the fact that Christ himself was a bachelor. Christ's urging to his disciples to leave everyone behind and follow him has been interpreted literally by the Catholic Church. Surely, though, leaving behind the richness of intimate relationships, sexuality, marriage and children is an unnecessary sacrifice which benefits no one, and which creates separation in many cases, depriving genuinely capable men of the flexibility of choice.

This suppression of normal masculinity, including sexual intimacy, has had other consequences. The use of physical violence by Catholic priests in grade schools and high schools was very common during much of this century. This abuse, often directed at boys who had misbehaved in Church or in the classroom, has had profound effects on young men, who continue to feel the consequences well into adulthood. Perhaps having abandoned the possibility of expressing virility through intimate relationships, one unfortunate alternative for the priest was to express it through physical or psychological domination and control over his subordinates. As a means of compensating, then, some priests went overboard in the direction of using violence, so as to be able to see themselves as "real" men. This was exacerbated by the general belief that suffering, punishment and subjugation of the will is intrinsically valuable: in this way, the priest becomes the agent of the Old Testament God, beating fear and respect into the boys. This Old Testament God felt rage and wrath, and expressed it in a direct way. The fact that physical violence is antithetical to the teachings of the Gospels seemed not to have occurred to many priests—although it may *well* have occurred to some of them, only serving to add to their own feelings of shame and guilt at the end of the day. Of course some priests were never involved in abuse of any type; but the fact remains that many individuals I interviewed did have experiences of abuse, too many to be ignored. When asked about his life in a Catholic boys high school, Mark said the following:

"There were boys being abused every day that I was there. They were hit in different ways: hand open, hand closed into a fist. Rulers and pointers were used on boys. Specially designed paddles were used. One paddle was known as 'the Educator', a long paddle with holes drilled into it which was supposed to sting more because it had holes. Someone would get caught and cuffed in class or would be sent to the disciplinarian. How's that for a job in a school? *Disciplinarian.* This was the guy who kicked ass. You saw it all over the place.

"Feelings? What I would remember most is that I would be ashamed. I couldn't let out any feelings of pain or sadness. I'd feel sissyish. That wasn't something that young men did. If I did start to feel things I'd feel ashamed and black it all out. I don't know how much of it was related to being a male and how much of it was related to being a *Catholic* male. I grew up in a Catholic household in the 60's and went to a Catholic grade school and high school so my impression of being a boy and man was very wrapped up in Catholicism. I remember I was shamed in both places for showing fear or crying. I would feel twice shamed. Better to just get beaten than to get beaten and cry. If it had happened in a public school the teacher would get thrown out of school for touching a kid. The idea at Catholic school was that if you didn't like it, you could get out—kind of like the Church!"

Another Catholic man described his high school experience in this way:

"I was never sexually approached by a priest but they did go in for physical things at my school. There was one priest who comes to mind. At seminary school they controlled kids through demerits. If you were late for Church, for example, you got demerits. One thing this one priest would do would be to give you the choice of a demerit or 'the grip', where he'd grab a hold of the fatty part of your stomach and squeeze as hard as he could. It was very painful. Everybody knew they had the option but nobody ever chose it a second time. There was another priest who was a good handball player. In the evenings you'd have to go to study hall for two hours and a lot of times you weren't interested and a lot of people would just open a book and try to take a nap, and if the priest caught you he'd sneak up behind you and use his handball approach and just swat you upside the head and knock your head into the desk. It wasn't like a priest would be angry and out of control but you were definitely disciplined through pain."

Unfortunately, many of us have numerous examples of abuse of this type, particularly in connection with Catholic schooling. While interviewing one recovering Catholic, I asked how he thought the priests running the schools would have rationalized the use of corporal punishment. His answer seemed consistent with many of the themes already presented:

"I think they would say that the Church needs strong, disciplined young men. They would say that the temptations of the world, the temptations of the flesh, run strong in young boys, and that sometimes young boys need not just a loving hand, but a firm hand, to grow up to be strong men. I think they'd also say that they would never intentionally injure a boy, and that any sufffering the boy would experience would be for his own good, and that was *nothing* compared to what Christ suffered, *for* him! (Laughs)."

In reviewing the experiences of both men and women, physical abuse towards men clearly dominated the scene. Incidents of sexual abuse towards boys was also an issue for a number of respondents. Several men also said they believed that some of the priests involved in physical abuse of students also derived sexual satisfaction from the incidents. An example of this *covert* sexual abuse can be seen in the observations of one respondent:

"A few years after we left school one of my best friends turned gay and walked into a bar on Chicago Avenue and ran into some of the brothers from high school. My friend reminded me that when we were in high school there was a whole group of brothers who used to sit and watch as we roughhoused in the pool, naked. I think it's pretty bizarre that on the surface they preached this 'party line' stuff, and all the time there was this gay faction operating. It was all incongruous."

And here is another example:

"I went to a Franciscan seminary to learn more about the priesthood when in high school. At the end of a weekend retreat I decided not to be a priest, an option I had been considering. The weekend had a definite sexual flavor. Maybe I was confused about it, being a young teenager and working out my identity, but it had an unforgettable feel to it. I remember not wanting any piece of it at the end, and it didn't have anything to do with God. It was uncomfortable, although nothing specific happened. I've never experienced anything sexually direct and inappropriate, with the exception of one brother, a Dominican at a religious camp, who was just too 'rubby', rubbing your back, rubbing arms and rubbing legs. He developed a following, and you were either one of his buddies or had nothing to do with him. In school I heard of boys who were stripped naked before they were spanked for misconduct, and I believe there was a sexual content to that."

This disparity, between the supposed moral superiority of priests, and their actual conduct in some cases, has played itself out in many areas of our Catholic background. The area of sexuality brings it to the surface in a way that is particularly distinctive and disturbing, because of the constant focus on purity, sin and misuse of the body. When a priest, who was seen as Christ's representative on earth, became sexual with a child or a teenager, or even with a young adult, the confusion was great. When I was in college in the 1970's the Church had undergone what it considered to be a transformation: we all went to guitar Masses, sang songs about peace, used bread at Communion time, and made banners out of felt which we hung up in Church. There was a spirit of renewal, and for those of us in the Church, it was a hopeful time. It was also at that time that priests were beginning to experiment with their own ideas and getting to know themselves, which in some cases meant experimenting with their sexuality. Had the powers that be been willing to look at the role of men and women in the Church in an open way, and to acknowledge the need for change in "the system", things might have been different. One survey respondent provided the following:

"I remember the feelings of disgust, confusion and fear that I experienced when I went to my student advisor at college; he had put pillows on the floor of his office and lit candles in an effort to 'get down to the students level'. While talking to him about my feelings about the Church, he suddenly leaned over and very roughly tried to French kiss me. I remembered thinking it was like kissing a little boy who had no experience with girls, and who felt the only way he would get what he wanted was through force. In retrospect, I feel a great deal of sadness for this man, for the denial of his sexuality, and for his personal inexperience in dealing with ordinary life."

Another female survey respondent adds her thoughts regarding college experience:

"In college I was enlightened about gender inequalities and hypocrisy in the Church, as I was witness to the behavior of priests in social settings and in positions of academic power over women. I saw many instances of priests being casual about their vows, and using their positions of power over women's academic careers to coerce sexual favors."

The following excerpt, by a non-Catholic, provides an "outsiders" view of the life within the priesthood, past and present:

"I haven't had much contact with Catholics, except through marriage, but I remember an experience that has stayed with me that involved a Catholic priest. I had a professional involvement with this particular priest, during the course of which I was invited over to the rectory for dinner. It was a large rectory, with three or four priests living there. The feeling I got was of a group of teenaged boys who were being waited on by their moms, in the form of the dedicated sisters. I had glimpses of shorts being ironed and meals being served and cleared by the sisters. The priests each had a room like a teenager would have, although some of the contents were different. There were bookcases with Paul Tillich and Teilhard de Chardin, and a stereo with Bach C.D.'s instead of heavy metal and comic books, but the feel was overpoweringly of adolescence, of lack of personal responsibility in the adult world as we think of it. My priest friend seemed a nice man, a very nice man, but undeveloped...."

PATRIARCHY

We were taught to respect all male clergy, with a clear understanding that the Pope, as head of the Church, was a special individual, personally supported and aided by God in an effort to care for his flock. We saw him as a spiritual king on earth, without human flaws as we knew them. He was always dressed beautifully as he stepped out onto the veranda at the Vatican and waved. The popes were interchangeable, with no individual personalities in the eyes of most Catholics. The issue of papal supremacy, along with the patriarchy of the Church in general, was a major issue for many of the former Catholics I interviewed. Although ordinary priests had limited power as compared to the pope, they were all capable of maintaining their own form of supremacy through various methods of limiting women's roles in the Church. One survey respondent made these comments:

"When I was a child, the full range of functions for women in the Church encompassed the convent, motherhood, or the Altar Society. Girls could not serve on the altar, could not attend Holy Name Society or Knights of Columbus meetings with their fathers and brothers, and would never be priest, bishop, or pope. I went to a Catholic girls' high school and despite years of heavy-duty questioning of clergy on doctrinal issues, engaged in the usual pious displays, but by the time I was a freshman the inequities began to seriously threaten my faith. I took a class taught by the American representative to the Ecumenical Council and his adamant conviction—that women could not be priests because Jesus was a man and it was tradition—insulted my intelligence and convinced me that organized religion was just another tool of the misogynist patriarchy. I can thank the Jesuits for making me a committed feminist."

As I approach the conclusion of this section, it would seem important to acknowledge the positive role that priests played in the lives of lay people. Unfortunately, few of these positive stories and experiences were forthcoming as the work progressed. The most upbeat ones came from the lives of people who were active in the Church in the late 60's and 70's, who remember workshops and retreats they attended with priests who were fun, lively, and who encouraged personal growth and thinking for oneself. They described these priests as warm, loving, and interested in creating a spirit of unity among the groups they were in. They also reported that they later discovered these same priests had often left the Church, unable to accept the Church's political or financial views, or because they wanted to be in the Church *and* be married, and were obviously unable to do both. It is ironic that *these* men, who were perhaps best able to able to represent both the human and the divine sides of our nature, were often the men who left the priesthood, and in many cases, left the Church. No doubt there were countless men in their 20's and 30's who would have made good priests, but who didn't consider it, due to the Church's inability to keep up with the needs of its time, and of its people.

THE ROLE OF WOMEN

In like fashion, Catholic families often felt special favor was being conferred on girls who decided they had a vocation. Consistent with society's views towards women, girls going into the convent were inferior to boys going into the priesthood. Girls were inferior to boys, nuns were inferior to priests. On a more generic level, this was clear to us, but for those of us who went to Catholic schools, the part played by nuns was a powerful one. While priests managed parishes and made occasional visits to school assemblies, the sisters were in charge of the day to day running of the school, and of our souls. Their job as "policewomen of the soul" involved scanning for possible occasions of sin, with the purpose of highlighting these in public; and sadly this often happened in a shaming way. While these women may well have thought they were acting with our best interests in mind, the use of fear as a learning tool is harmful and most often counterproductive. The worst experiences were described by interviewees discussing grade school days during the mid 1960's and before. Those in grade school in the later 60's and 70's typically said they didn't have that much experience with nuns, and that they had all lay teachers. Some respondents to the survey said they had positive experiences with sisters in the 60's and 70's, but that often these nuns had left the convent in order to get married or for other reasons.

For many of us, nuns were mysterious, magical creatures. Like priests, they dressed in different clothing from ours. Considerable speculation went into whether they wore black underwear, whether they went to the bathroom, and what they wore to bed at night. A cause of confusion was the wedding band they wore on their left hand. We were told the sisters were married to Christ. The Baltimore Catechism stated: "In the flesh Mary was his mother, but in the Spirit she was his bride". Doesn't this sound uncomfortably like incest? The confusion in roles, the sexual suppression re-emerging in the phrase "Mary, the Bride of Christ"; all of this seems indicative of a limited way of thinking, developed by human beings frightened to deal directly with their own sexuality. An elaborate story was created, involving conception without sexuality, intense non-sexual intimacy between mother and son, and a distant father, with no other siblings to interfere with this chaste picture. Our sexual fears, the fears of our parents, and the fears of the Church hierarchy itself made it possible for us to adopt these beliefs. In my work with troubled families, one of the most common family dynamics today is that of an overinvolved mother and child, and a distant father. Perhaps the emphasis on Jesus and his relationship with his mother—with Joseph very much in the background—is simply a reflection of dysfunctional family life throughout the centuries.

This denial of sexuality often gave nuns a sexless, joyless demeanor. The body was covered from head to toe in black. Keys, handkerchiefs, and holy medals were all hidden away, to be pulled out in a private moment. For most of us, the hands and faces of sisters were all we saw of them.

The role of significant women in the Gospels, like Mary, Martha and Veronica, was essentially a subservient one, reflecting the cultural bias of the time. These women were portrayed as servants waiting for events to happen in order to respond, as opposed to being active, dynamic forces in their own right. They seemed to have no personal power of their own. In thinking back to childhood experiences, it is ironic that many of us had women teachers who were dragons in the classroom, yet became sweet and ingratiating whenever a priest came into the room. The narrowness of their role definition, and their small amount of actual capacity to influence the "powers that be" in the Church seem a good explanation for their abuse of power in the classroom. Like priests, their belief in the rightness of punishment and suffering supported their actions. One interview subject described his experience in this way:

"Sister M. was the principal in our school near Seattle. She would walk around monitoring classes while they were going on, and I could tell it made the other nuns very nervous. She would walk down the rows and if you were doing something wrong she would grab your earlobe and twist it, as she continued walking, and pull you out of your desk, before eventually letting go. Then she'd walk down the next row and do it to someone else and then walk on, never saying what it was that you'd done. This ear thing happened with me and my brother and sister, also. It was scary and confusing, since it wasn't connected to any specific 'crime'—just random attack. Three years ago, as a 34 year-old man, I saw her in the hospital where my father was dying. I was with my brother, and was surprised that she had recognized him. I really wanted to confront her but was so much in shock at seeing her, and so upset about my Dad, that I didn't do it."

Another told this story:

"In grade school, some of us in the back corner of the room were goofing off. The sister stopped the class and demanded to know who was responsible. No one stood up. She had the entire back corner of the room go out in the hall and kneel on our hands for the rest of the class. That was perhaps half an hour. It was very painful. Many kids had bruised or swollen fingers. Some were bleeding from the bits of gravel or such on the floor. When we complained to another nun in the hallway she told us to offer up the suffering to God."

Not all forms of abuse are physical, of course. I came across many stories in which nuns exercised a certain sadistic power over our youthful imaginations. Here is a telling example:

"One incident of cruelty that stands out in my mind is a nun's description of purgatory and hell to our class of young children. She was both graphic and eloquent. She described the pain and the smell and the sight of burning flesh, and the screams, which would of course not be heard. This was inevitably waiting for us and our families and friends to atone to God, our Father, for our stained souls—our imperfect selves."

In listening to recovering Catholics tell their stories about verbal and physical abuse by nuns, the same questions were repeated time and time again. Where did they learn to be so mean? Who trained them to be that way? How were they trained? Recently I read a book by a Catholic author who boiled it all down to P.M.S. This theory provides a unique but seriously limited explanation of the sisters' behavior, which did *not* last 5 to 10 days a month, but was constant. Many of the stories told to me were similar, with methods of punishment repeated time and again in classrooms all around the country. It was as though a monthly newsletter had been sent from convent to convent informing sisters of new techniques for punishment! Several respondents said they had been tempted to talk to their former teachers about the "bad old days" but found that the sisters had changed and were essentially "nice *now*," prompting a decision to forget about it. No doubt these same sisters dislike looking back also, resulting in a generalized, unspoken agreement to put it all under the carpet.

This hesitation to "stir up the pot" showed up often in my interviews:

"Speaking for myself, the thought of confronting a nun stirs up major fear. The greatest fear is not of being angrily put in my place, but of having to face that wry, patronizing laugh or look, like I was being childish and imagining things; or I might get vague answers to my questions that *sounded* good but were essentially bullshit. Then I'd somehow be left taking the responsibility for *their* behavior, and I'd end up feeling even more shameful than before. It just doesn't seem worth it."

This pattern is similar to one I see regularly in working with survivors of sexual abuse. The survivor in adult life is often fearful of confronting the perpetrator for fear that the abuse will be denied or minimized, and that they will just end up being retraumatized in some way. For recovering Catholics, working with these issues more actively is definitely an option; this will be discussed more in Section II.

Although fearful events seem to dominate many former Catholics' contact with nuns, sometimes contrasting feelings of awe, wonder, and affection were intermingled, which could be confusing:

> "In third grade we had a nun who was so excited about teaching but she got in trouble with her superiors for laughing. She had *too much spirit*; I remember her being so loving."

And this:

> "In college I was almost overwhelmed with the beautiful atmosphere. The nuns were charming and caring and loving and I really felt that, after so many years as a Catholic in public school, I was finally among my own people. Back then, everyone understood the same rules and we all felt superior. It was great!"

In the 1960's the sisters' role expanded, as dress was modernized and many nuns began to live in houses and apartments. With these changes came a new awareness of personal feminine power. Some nuns left the convent and/or the Church, as did many priests, and went on to work for change in the still male-dominated hierarchy of the Church. A good number of them began campaigning for the ordination of women priests, for a change in the Catholic stance regarding birth control (particularly as it effected third world countries), and even for pro-choice on the abortion issue. These same sisters often worked to change liturgies that appear sexist, and strived to connect with other organizations and Churches in ways that were not acceptable to the Vatican; for example, they might attend an Episcopal Church and receive Communion and invite members of that church to receive Communion at a Catholic Mass. Although some of the former Catholics I interviewed were aware of these changes, they still expressed continued confusion about nuns' motivation and behavior. Here is the Past and Present list of statements from former Catholics regarding nuns:

PAST	PRESENT
Nuns were the "handmaidens" of the Church. Good for baking hosts, sewing altar cloths, and teaching kids for free. I was in appropriate awe of nuns—they had a lot of power over us. When I was eight years old I thought about being a nun (temporary insanity!)	The slaves of the Church. Willing participants in their own enslavement. They do much more concrete good for social justice than priests. Should all vote with their feet and get out of an abusive system.
Nuns were more holy than the rest of us. God likes them more.	Nuns are a reinforcement of marriage and sex as evil and sinful.

Feared them. Thought they knew everything. Tried to be good.	Celibacy should be optional—then they'd be in the world. Today I respect nuns much more than most priests.
"Holy people", "married to God", almost never sinned or did anything wrong.	Ordinary people. Some are maladjusted.
God's representatives.	In the present form, a waste of good lives.
In my school, they acted as God the Father—full of wrath and rage for the most part.	I think many of them are pretty powerful women in the sense of advocating change, but they are still accepting old values like celibacy.

Clearly, the roles assumed by the clergy, both male and female, had a strong, profound and long-term effect in many of our lives. Some present-day Catholic authors discourage us from looking too closely at the effects of this background, reminding us that problems we experience in adult life may have been just as influenced by the family upbringing we received. While this is certainly true, we must also remember that our parents were *Catholic* parents, who generally seem to have supported whatever the Church thought appropriate, who saw the clergy as having more wisdom, and who also may have interpreted the rules of the Church in bizarre and inappropriate ways, by essentially overidentifying with and conforming to the rigidity of the Catholic system. Part of the healing process is to openly and clearly examine both the useful *and* the fearful aspects of our relationships with the clergy, so as to honor the past and to move on. Hopefully, we will ultimately be able to do this with a spirit of compassion for those who were our teachers, as they were also the product of the same type of upbringing. We can acknowledge this without in any way minimizing the abuse we received or its influence in our lives.

SECTION II
HEALING

Chapter Seven
GETTING STARTED

*T*here is no "right" way to do this work. It is important to emphasize this since, as little Catholic girls and boys, there was always a correct way to do everything, a way that was "pleasing to God". Similarly, there were many people and situations that would lead us "away from God" and into sin. There was no middle ground, but that is exactly where we need to be if we are going to facilitate healing and achieve a sense of balance. It is completely acceptable to experiment with a variety of healing tools. It is good for the inner child to get the message that exploration, creativity and sometimes messiness are all parts of the process. No one will be judging this, calling it good or bad. We are doing this work entirely for ourselves. It is helpful to do it for the enjoyment of the process itself, rather than because it's going to get us somewhere. Much of our childhood was devoted to upholding specific codes of behavior so that we would later be with God in heaven. Now we can simply take delight in our own step-by-step changing.

The process itself is unique for each of us. Some of us may love to write and will work best with reams of paper. Others may talk, draw, work with clay, dance, study, meditate or use music as an aid to change. We might combine various tools or alternate them as our mood dictates. There is room for humor, creativity, silliness. For our purposes, the greater the flexibility in our mode of changing the better, allowing us to move beyond the rigid and rule-bound conventions of the past.

Although the freedom to work in ways that are useful to you may sound inviting to the adult part of yourself, the inner child may not be as enthusiastic, and may come up with a lot of reasons to avoid working out a plan that best represents your needs, desires, and special talents and interests. As former Catholics, it is particularly easy to avoid working on this, because many of us have had no significant contact with Catholicism, nor does it typically occupy our thoughts in day to day life; so that when the inner child balks and suggests that we simply forget it, it's easy to go along, particularly as the adult part of ourselves already has plenty of other things to do. One solution to this problem is to put aside regular time in a given day or week, to be devoted to "Catholic" work. In this way, you have prioritized the work and given it a consistent place in your schedule. This doesn't mean you may not continue to feel resistance coming from your inner child, but scheduling time will help prepare for the resistance, and enable you to manage it successfully. As you move through the next few chapters, give yourself permission to develop and work with what fits for you. Design a plan that incorporates exercises you see as most useful, changing and adapting the plan as you continue to do the work. Most of us need to incorporate greater flexibility into our lives in general. Adapting a healing plan regularly allows us increased feelings of control and self-respect, feelings that our inner child will thrive on.

Moving beyond the limitations and restraints of our Catholic past is a lifelong journey. Essentially there are three steps in this process:

1. Identifying.

This is allowing ourselves to *name*, to become conscious of, the core beliefs and experiences that have become an integral (although often unwelcome) part of our thinking, feelings lives. Some of these are easy to identify because they have remained close to the surface; others may be deeply buried, long since forgotten but still operating as subtle but potent forces. It is important to be watchful for a particular kind of resistance here: the kind that says: "God! this is so *negative!* Isn't it time to let all this stuff go?" Yes, it is. But contrary to what some self-help books would have us believe, it really isn't possible to let go of something, if we haven't allowed ourselves to truly bring to awareness exactly what it is that needs to be let go of. Often I have had clients who think that they have forgiven their parents, for example—"they did the best they could, based on what they knew and understood at the time"—but who still find themselves filled with unresolved feelings of anger and hurt. All too often they have not allowed themselves to bring their feelings, thoughts and memories fully into awareness. I have come to see this as a kind of premature forgiveness, and it is quite different from the deep acceptance that can come later as a *natural* result of a more complete healing process.

2. Releasing.

Releasing is the conscious and intentional act of letting go of ideas and patterns from the past in order to make room for healthier beliefs.

3. Replacing.

This is the act of replacing old unwanted beliefs and experiences with more life-affirming and nourishing ones. This can be both a conscious and an unconscious process: some "new growth" will be the result of deliberate and disciplined choice-making, and some will take the form of unexpected and often delightful changes in attitude and awareness.

There are many different ways to approach this process of Identifying, Releasing and Replacing. One tool that I have found to be particularly powerful is the use of a mirror to access our inner beliefs, emotions and experiences.

MIRROR WORK

Mirror work essentially involves sitting and looking at ourselves in a mirror and having our reflection represent a certain part or parts of our personality: for example, the child, the teenager, or the young adult. This process allows us to enter into a dialogue with ourselves. It is one technique among many of getting in touch with parts of ourselves that may otherwise be difficult to access.

Looking into a mirror can be frightening to many of us. Our eyes bring us into the center of ourselves. "The eyes are the mirrors of the soul". The eyes hold the truth about who we are and who we *think* we are. They also capture and remind us of all that we despise about ourselves. Critical voices insist on our inadequacies as soon as we begin to listen closely. Our criticism of our face, grey hair, blemishes and wrinkles are simply surface manifestations of deeper feelings of unworthiness, learned much earlier on. But Mirror work can take us past this shame-based morass to a deeper and infinitely more accepting part of ourselves.

Mirror work is referred to at several points throughout the healing section and specific suggestions will be made at these points regarding how to use it.

IDENTIFYING

Use a Bible, an old Missal, a Baltimore Catechism or any other older Catholic books, magazines, or pamphlets, leafing through them in order to find words, sentences and phrases that feel very negative to you, or that stir up old unpleasant memories. Write these down along with the feelings or memories. You might also want to simply sit back quietly with eyes closed, feet on the floor, phone turned off, and no other distractions, and allow ideas to come into your mind without the use of an aid. Both methods have their advantages. Using old visual aids is particularly helpful in reminding you of what the Church actually said, while the visualization method helps you get in touch with your own experience. (The focus on this exercise is on memories and issues that feel unpleasant and unfinished. In a later chapter we'll work with positive memories and feelings.)

A warning at this point seems appropriate: this exercise may feel uncomfortable or distressing. This discomfort is *not* the goal of the exercise, although some may be tempted to see it as such. At the same time, it's useful to *observe* whatever we feel.

One client provided the following journal excerpt:

"At this moment, as I write, I feel my neck stiffen up. I feel slightly tearful. I feel tense, and on the verge of a headache. I know that what I'm about to write comes from another part of myself. I feel nervous that this part is going to take over somehow. I have kids to pick up in 2 hours. Is it possible to do this in bits and pieces? I cannot believe I have a 4th grader and I'm dealing with these things that happened to *me* in 4th grade. I'm worried I might lose the 'Mom' part of myself".

She then continued the exercise by compiling a list of memories, thoughts and feelings in a way that made the most sense for her. Here is her list:

IDENTIFYING LIST

- I have black marks on my soul.
- I remember my continued, abiding fear of the Confessional. It was so dark, and reminded me of what hell would probably be like. Also, it had a strange smell that scared me.
- I remember a priest having a sexual relationship with a girl at my school. I felt very confused, but also scared (because I wasn't supposed to know); also, scared that something bad would happen to her and that it might be my fault for not telling. On the other hand I thought "Since he's a priest, maybe there's something I'm not understanding".
- I had the feeling of just being "bad" no matter what I do.
- I felt panic a lot thinking I was probably about to do something wrong.
- I had a feeling of panic that I was not doing my penance right.
- I remember feeling so scared looking at my grade school prinicipal's face. She looked so sinister, and it was always the same look. She forced me to look into her face if I averted my eyes.
- I feel anger *now*, remembering being inappropriately touched myself by a priest when I was 17 years old. I remember feeling shock and disbelief *then*.

It's very helpful to simply accept your own feelings, to move at your own speed, to trust the adult part of yourself to remain "in charge", and to see your feelings as a natural part of the process. Your so-called negative reactions are simply a form of questioning on the part of your deeper self, alerting you to the fact that you are doing something out of the ordinary here, and is this *really* what you want to be doing? It's like the little box that you see on your computer just before you are about to erase some material, emphasizing in bold exclamation points that this is about to happen: "Are you *sure* you wish to delete the file 'Immaculate Misconceptions?'" This warning may take the form of some type of physical reaction, it may be expressed through strong feeling, or it may take the form of denial: when unpleasant experiences or ideas are pushed down unconsciously where they can no longer cause pain in daily life. For many children this was an effective means of coping. With more knowledge, maturity and understanding now available to us we can choose to raise some of these specters from the dead, aware that we can look at them directly and dispel them. Still, some of our work may be slow in evolving, as though we are waking from a dream. One interviewee, who attended Catholic schools all the way through high school, and whose parents were strict Catholics, described his denial in this way:

"I looked through your questionnaire and some of the terms and it didn't even look familiar! I knew it was something religious, something that should have been in my past. I figured it was pretty good repression. It goes with other things from my childhood. I have a hard time remembering a lot of things successfully. It seems as though it was necessary for me to put things aside. When the stuff does come up it's like somebody else's life."

The important thing here is the fact that this man is willing to look at what is going on. Simply accepting the denial at face value is useful in the process of letting go. It is also important to be aware that you may not agree with what you have just written regarding your own experience. It may seem childish, silly, or simply *not true* in the eyes of your adult self. Acknowledge the fact that you and the deeper child part may see things differently. This does not make you "schizophrenic" as some people might fear. It simply means you are a rich and varied individual who is at times conflicted and confused.

Exploring personal beliefs regarding spiritual matters such as dogma, doctrine and traditions, provides a further means of identifying the issues. It can be very helpful to look honestly at the specific beliefs and traditions you no longer adhere to. Here is one client's list:

THINGS I NO LONGER BELIEVE

- Jesus Christ was God's only Son.
- He descended into Hell.
- The body will be resurrected.
- Christ died for our sins.
- God is "just", meaning that some people are going to get His "wrath".
- Hell, and anything to do with the devil.
- Only men should be priests.
- The Catholic Church is the One True Church.
- "Sins" are bad.

As you do this work, you may find there are some beliefs and traditions which leave a question mark in your mind. Remember it is okay to be messy, to be unsure, to feel up in the air. It is helpful to write down these uncertain beliefs and put them on the back burner for a later date. Here is one client's example:

UNCERTAIN LIST

- God created the earth.
- The Resurrection.
- Eternal life (heaven).
- Value of celibacy.
- Prayers are answered.

Take time to compile these lists. For many Catholics the feelings of resentment can act as a solid block, inhibiting you from separating old beliefs from the emotional trappings which accompanied them. This particular task may be easier for those of you who have recently left the Church, because you may be more in touch with your beliefs. Others will have a harder time getting through the blocks that may have been erected over time, but persistence will pay off.

By the time you have finished, you should have a fairly sizeable master list to work from, and which can be added to. These phrases, ideas, sentences, memories, emotions and beliefs are your spiritual buttons which, when pushed, help to unlock deeper feelings which may have remained dormant for a number of years. Keep in mind that having a good laugh at a party, and swapping horror stories about being raised Catholic, does not necessarily mean that these experiences have been dealt with. Your inner child retains the memory *and* the emotional baggage.

RELEASING

The next step is to take these spiritual buttons and work with them. This can be called the releasing stage. The basic idea is to consciously express a desire to let go of this particular belief, teaching, or memory, with the full expectation that some type of inward change is going to occur as a result. The focus at this point, however, is not on the change, but on the letting go. It is simply the recognition that the particular belief is not working any longer: it is a spiritual dinosaur, hanging around without a useful purpose but clogging up your "ecosystem" nonetheless. As young Catholics we saw God as being "in charge", as doling out treats as He saw fit, and depriving us or punishing us for reasons unknown to us. A changing view of the situation acknowledges that we ourselves have more power than we take credit for, and that one form of power is the ability to unravel and discard what doesn't work in our lives.

There are a number of ways of doing clearing work using the mirror. Jeff, a recovering Catholic, described the following:

"I was doing some mirror work, and the image of Sister R. came to me. There she was, glaring and looking as mean

111

as she did in second grade. I started hearing all this stuff from her, asking me how Jesus would feel if he saw me talking in class. I just let her talk but imagined seeing all the words come out of her mouth, like a Callahan cartoon, and watched them drop into the garbage can next to her desk."

The use of a more ritualized style of clearing works well for some people. You could simply look into the mirror and say "I let go of my belief in the devil, I let go of my belief in Hell, I let go of memories of the image of Purgatory."

Talking aloud to the inner child can be the most direct way to clear old blockages, because the child holds the memories and feelings intact. It can be useful here to dig up some old childhood photographs of yourself as a way of bringing to life the person you were. You can see the child you once were in the mirror and talk to him or her, allowing the child to tell you what makes them mad, what feels scary, sad, or worried, about God, or the Church. Don't assume that because you no longer hold these beliefs as an adult, little will be forthcoming. One recovering Catholic (a present-day atheist) was shocked to hear her inner child tell her that the reason she didn't want to call her mother more often was for fear that her mother would make veiled comments about her not going to Mass anymore, *and that she still felt guilty!*

On a practical level, you may feel most comfortable initially letting the child speak aloud for a few minutes, and then responding for a few minutes. This allows each of you to get warmed up. Please don't give up after trying for 30 seconds. It's important to give yourself time to get used to this idea, as it will naturally feel awkward. Keep your expectations intentionally vague, and give yourself credit for any small shifts that occur in your understanding. In time, it will become easier to do and you will become aware of changes more quickly.

For some, this type of work is embarrassing, even when done

alone. It can also feel strange having different parts of yourself relate out loud. Again, keep in mind these feelings are common and normal, and need not be a deterrent. Just keep working, and if you start having thoughts like "This is silly", or "I must be crazy", remind yourself that various parts are always present in you anyway. This is simply a more direct way of hearing those parts, that allows you a clearer sense of control. More choices will become available to you as the work continues.

When talking to the child part of yourself, use the skills you may already have as a parent, grandparent, aunt or uncle. Use language that is on the same level as the child. If you are talking to a part that seems like a teenager, use language geared to an older child. When talking to a younger part of yourself, use language appropriate to that age. Reach inside yourself to get a sense of distinction between the child and adult parts. Keep in mind that it is possible (with some practice) to really get a conversation going in which both parts have an opportunity to express themselves. At the beginning you may be unclear about who is who. Don't let this uncertainty, as strange as it may feel, keep you from continuing to experiment.

Sometimes our body will act as a barometer of our internal emotional state; for this reason, we are often able to access repressed feelings by intentionally tuning in to our body signals. While looking in the mirror, remain alert to feelings of tension in the muscular system and also aware of inner changes (for example, with pulse and respiration). One client noted her observations:

"I looked in the mirror to find my shoulders slumped down in the way they have done since childhood, whenever I feel guilt and shame. I also noted a worried look in the eyes and a furrowed brow. I said: 'I release all tension in my body. I let go of worry, I let go of any old ideas I may be carrying that relate to questioning the authority of the Church. I let go of the idea of sacrilege.' "

While speaking it is helpful to feel aware of increased relaxation or change of posture and to be aware that many feelings may surface as the work progresses. They may be related feelings (sadness and loneliness) or mixed feelings (angry and joyful). The reason for this is that the releasing process may trigger several memories at the same time, or the feelings may have been mixed at the time of the experience. One Catholic client said he remembered feeling ashamed and aroused simultaneously when confessing the "sin" of masturbation. Simply allow the feelings to come up, then work on detaching from them, while watching them as an observer. This may seem somewhat cold, but remember that in one sense you are no longer the child you once were, and the feelings can be viewed the same way in which you might watch an old movie. It is helpful to keep in mind (when you, the adult, feel shocked or disturbed by the feelings that come up) that these are the feelings of a 5 or 10 or 16 year-old, and that the concerns and fears of a child can be handled by a loving adult who is thoughtful about how to work with that particular child. Here is an example of how the issue of feeling simultaneously ashamed and aroused during Confession was resolved:

"What I didn't know back then was that feeling aroused just through hearing a word like 'sex' is not an uncommon thing for a man, and certainly would not be strange or uncommon for a 16 year-old boy. I know now, in fact, that it is a pretty normal response, no matter what the context. This type of education is what that teenaged part of myself needed. I did some talking into the mirror and some guilt and embarrassment came up, while I just continued to talk about it, reassuring myself that masturbation is a healthy thing, and that I can actually feel proud that I am enjoying my body that way. I still feel some of that guilt, but I also feel like I am getting through, that I am starting to have some weight with that part of myself."

Simply talking aloud to the kid part or letting her talk to you while driving a car or working at home alone can be helpful. Imaginative means of releasing, tailor-made to suit you, will work the best, because they will honor the uniqueness that makes up the person you are. Ideas for how to do this will occur to you as you embrace the process. One client who enjoyed working with clay made a sculpture depicting her childhood fear of going to hell. She lived with it for several days, then smashed it, symbolizing her willingness to let go of her fear. She found this satisfying in two ways, because she also felt guilty as a child whenever she expressed anger. Another client wrote out particularly disturbing experiences on slips of paper, went to a nearby river, threw them in, and watched them float away from her, mindful of the pleasure inherent in releasing them.

REPLACING

The work of the third stage is to replace thought, memory, or belief with healthier new ideas and experiences. After doing his clearing work with Sister R., Jeff decided to have her treat him the way he would have liked to have been treated in the past. He looked in the mirror and saw her looking at him in a kinder way, and heard her speak to him respectfully. Even though the situation or belief is from the past and obviously cannot be changed, an *emotional* correction can always be initiated, which can have a significant impact on that particular issue. The way in which the correction is made is up to you and calls for some intuitive thought. If it's not clear to you how to proceed, stop and come back to it at a later time when you're feeling more inspired.

In replacing belief and thought we need to go back to the list of old outdated beliefs, replacing each one with a new belief that best demonstrates our thinking *at the present time.* Just as our beliefs have changed from past to present, they will also change from present to future. Seeing beliefs as fluid and adaptable in and of itself helps to heal the rigidity of the past.

Many of us grew up believing that all doctrine, tradition and moral teachings put forth by the Church were true unconditionally; this is a belief that will need to be brought to the surface where it can be challenged by you. The exercise assumes that the locus of control, in your beliefs and in your life, rests with you. If accepting this idea causes difficulty, air the difficulty with yourself openly. Before compiling his list of revised beliefs, one client heard a priestly voice in his head say the following: "What makes you think you can act on your own behalf in matters of faith? If each person dictated their own beliefs there wouldn't be a Catholic Church. These beliefs have been given to the people by God through Christ. Who are you to contradict them? This is a very dangerous precedent." He needed to respond to that "priestly" part of himself before he could honestly look at his beliefs. He needed to take responsibility for the fact that the thoughts were now coming from inside himself. Simply dismissing the voice and hoping it would magically correct itself would have been useless. It would have represented a child-like fantasy that somehow the adults would straighten themselves out and that things would change, while he remained passive, waiting.

Despite the fact that we are no longer in the Church, many of us are aware that we still have controlling spiritual voices in our heads, usually rigid in nature and set on redirecting our thinking away from an honest and open look at our beliefs. These voices represent that part of our Catholic experience which was limited and guilt-inducing. They are critical and complaining voices. They are judgmental and unwilling to respect or value uniqueness. Sometimes these voices are so muted that we are not aware of their influence in our lives. They become background music that influences us in subtle ways, even without our knowledge. We need to turn the volume up so that we clearly hear what they have to say, then decide how we want to respond. While doing this exercise, my client answered these inner voices in this way: "Look, I'm writing down some things that lots of people might feel but are too scared to say. If they're already thinking these things or other things that concern them, it's not good for this stuff to be kept shoved down inside. Maybe some of these old ideas need to be looked at. Anyway, you're not God. What are *you* frightened of?" At this point he felt better and was able to compile his own list.

Another way to deal with the resistance is to role play. Find another Catholic friend who would be willing to play the role of "the Church" as we knew it in childhood, or the way it is today, if you choose. Talk back and forth with that person as a means of clarifying your own thoughts. Be in touch with your inner child and aware of his or her feelings. As you gain confidence in yourself, prepare for the work of replacing your old beliefs with new ones. This may increase your feeling of confidence in working with the child alone in mirror work.

In order to change beliefs, take out your list and spend time considering each belief carefully, then write a new one. This process may take some time. For some it may be a simple exercise but revealing, nonetheless, because it represents the core of your spiritual life at present. One former Catholic wrote the following:

WHAT I BELIEVE AT PRESENT

- Every person is the Son and Daughter of God (i.e. I don't believe in Christ as exclusive).
- Christ was conceived in a human way.
- Hell is a figment of our imagination.
- The body is a vehicle for learning.
- Christ died to show there is no death.

- God does not get angry—this is a human emotion.
- There is no devil, except as represented symbolically by the things we think that hurt us.
- Spirituality is anything that makes me feel I'm growing from the inside out.
- Every Church is the One True Church.
- I embrace all parts of my self, including all that I dislike about myself, knowing that as I do, these parts will take shape and achieve purpose.

Keep in mind that this list will of course be unique to the individual, and will most likely change over time.

The process covered in this chapter—identifying beliefs, releasing them, and replacing those beliefs—can be used in an isolated way, in regard to specific issues, or can be used in a more extensive way, depending on the amount of interest and motivation you have in doing the work. Many people decide to begin with one or two beliefs, and to work with those until confidence grows. There is no "correct" way to do the work. Like all other aspects of healing work, you do what you are able or willing to do. It is very important to praise yourself for every piece of work you do. The *amount* is not the issue. If you start by simply looking at yourself in the mirror, support yourself for this first piece of work. Perfection is not an issue either. Keep in mind that this is valuable whatever you now consider yourself to be: a practicing member of a Church or other spiritual program, an agnostic, or an atheist.

Some recovering Catholics will fall into this work easily and effortlessly and others will grow into it gradually. As I've said, there is no "right" way. Those who typically express themselves in quieter ways may want to initially focus on the written aspects of these exercises, and do mirror work more slowly, while those who feel comfortable with the mirror may want to incorporate the two more quickly.

CHAPTER EIGHT

BODY WORK

very Ash Wednesday we heard a priest say: "Remember man that you are dust, and to dust you shall return". Many of us strongly believed that the body is insignificant in comparison to the spirit, and some of us put this belief into practise by fasting even beyond the required number of hours, thereby depriving ourselves of necessary sustenance. By having us keep our hands behind our backs, Sr. J. taught that punishment and suffering of the body was a small price to pay for the salvation of our immortal souls. In many Catholic schools altar boys were taught to maintain strict body postures during Mass, despite heat, fatigue, and illness. If they questioned this they were told to "offer it up". Christ's suffering on the Cross was often used as a reminder, creating feelings of guilt for even *feeling* their own "petty" discomfort.

Healing through body work is helpful in dealing with the embarrassment, shame and humiliation that so often warped our body image. Body work can help us become aware of the beauty and magnificence of our physical selves. A number of Eastern and Western practices and treatments can help both in releasing old feelings *and* developing this sense of appreciation: practices such as rolfing, reiki, interpretive dance, massage, biofeedback, t'ai chi, stretching and yoga. While those I've mentioned are currently popular, *any* physical activity which feels physically invigorating is useful. One client who enjoys golf described the following:

> "I would go out and play golf and even though I'm a fairly decent golfer, I would keep berating myself throughout the whole thing, putting down my arm, my swing, the fact that I was out there on the course rather than doing the lawn, you name it. One day I just decided to apply some of this to my game. I just let every swing of the club stand for letting go of all that *guilt*. It was actually pretty satisfying".

Any work which helps you appreciate your body and its great capacity for giving and receiving love, for enduring despite obstacles, for healing itself, or for accommodating the demands placed on it over time, can be richly rewarding. Choose what feels most interesting and most inviting, and let yourself be creative about ways of representing release through that particular activity. One recovering Catholic recounted this story:

> "Some years ago I attended a women's self-defense class. At the final class we were all instructed on how to put our fist through a board. I was very scared to do this, scared of my own power and scared to hurt myself. I allowed the board to represent *the fear itself*, while breaking the board symbolized my ability to smash through it successfully, and unscathed. I now have the two pieces of broken board mounted on the wall (where the Crucifix might have been!) as a trophy."

Body work can be especially useful for those of us who tend to store unexpressed feelings in our bodies. In my experience, former

Catholics who were particularly serious and unquestioning of the Church's teaching regarding the body and suffering seem more prone to holding feelings in, and are much more likely to experience bodily tension as a result, whereas those who went right ahead and played, danced, and sang jubilantly (without guilt) seem to have less tendency to retain feelings in this way. Many of us, of course, fit into the "grey area": we are healthier in relation to certain body issues than others.

The type of body work you choose depends on a number of different factors: age, weight, agility, desire, time commitment, life experience, and physical capacity. It is helpful to remember that resistance is just as likely here as it has been in the other work. If you are able to anticipate it, it will obstruct you less. My client who loves to play golf began to realize that he often sabotaged his attempts to schedule golf games because it was essentially too much fun, and there was not enough pain. He began to look at how he had used his body over the years and discovered he had often overexerted himself in any number of ways, resulting in long-term tendon and muscle damage in different parts of the body. He had learned to push himself in his adolescence after receiving a considerable amount of physical abuse in a Catholic grade school. With the knowledge that golf wasn't "painful enough" he was able to take special precautions to ensure that his golf game went as planned. Enjoying himself was uncomfortable at first, but this is an element in all body work. Our Catholic teachings essentially said: "If it feels good, don't do it!" The antithesis to this, of course, is "If it feels bad, that is good, although that is nothing compared to Christ's suffering." For this reason, it is important to monitor your own body work, looking not only for possible resistance in the form of balking, but also, resistance in the form of pushing yourself beyond your own capacity and endurance.

SEXUALITY

According to our Catholic teachings, we were to love one another as we love ourselves. Maybe I was absent that day, but I don't remember being taught how to love myself in a *general* way, much less in a specific way, through the use of my body in sexuality. Sexual mores and codes of behavior taught us to fear our own bodies and the bodies of others. I remember a period in the early 1980's when stage plays such as 'Patent Leather Shoes Really Do Reflect Up' were popular. These plays got a lot of laughs, partly because we all remembered situations in our lives similar to those depicted on stage. But there is usually more to these memories than the laughter would suggest; as one interviewee recalled:

"When I was in 8th grade, Sr. S. divided the class into two groups. The boys went with Father B. and the girls stayed behind with her. She got really serious and austere and went on to give us the only formal sex education we were to receive; it consisted of the following advice:

1) Keep apples near the door after a date. If a boy tries to kiss you, start chomping on the apple to avoid being kissed.

2) Never eat ravioli on a date. It reminds a boy of pillows and may lead to impure thoughts and desires.

3) Patent leather shoes *do* reflect up.

"This information, in combination with some written material on the advantages of wearing underpants to bed (as a means of avoiding impure thoughts) constituted the only solid data I had on what the future would hold regarding sexuality. I also got certain clear understandings through the tone of voice and body language of nuns and priests in religion class: that sexuality was not okay, and that purity is highly desirable. Later in life, when no longer a Catholic, I remember feeling an emotional burden lifted when I saw the movie 'The Last Temptation of Christ', which portrayed

Jesus as a sexual being who used his body in a loving way. I don't know if the New Testament authors would have considered that a demeaning representation of Christ. For me, it enhanced a feeling of connection with Jesus as a person."

IDENTIFYING

There are many ways of working on sexual healing. Again, the first step is to simply identify what the inner child or teenager sees as "impure". You can do this by means of mirror work, by having a conversation with him or her, or by letting the child write to you about the body and it's meaning. Don't be surprised if some time or effort is needed in order for the child to feel comfortable talking about this. While many non-Catholics have hang-ups about sexual acts, the Catholic teaching was that not only were sexual acts outside of marriage unacceptable, deliberate sexual *thoughts* were, too. Many children simply learned to back away from the whole issue, becoming deeply conflicted about how and with whom to discuss it.

In listening to the child, or teenager, you may become aware of certain target words that tend to elicit feelings of guilt or embarrassment. Try to focus on these and get an understanding of where these feelings originated. Resist any temptation to resist temptation! Simply go right into the center of these feelings. If you get stuck, use free association to loosen yourself up: take a piece of paper and write down anything that comes to mind as it relates to the body and sexuality. Stop when you can't think of anything else to include. Trust that what you have written stems from very real feelings you may have denied for some time. Having isolated some of the repressed areas, you can begin to make decisions about how to deal with them. In some cases, a professional counselor, spouse, or friend may be a helpful assistant in your work to let go of limited thinking. For many people, the sexual area is confusing and frightening, with a variety of thoughts and feelings competing for top billing. For all of us, time and patience is necessary to unravel the confused elements. If this feels difficult, working with another person can help provide a sense of perspective.

Keep in mind that some of what you have written may be useful and enriching, while some of it may feel dated and unnecessary. It's up to you to decide what you want to keep and what you want to release. Here is a list provided by a client who completed the exercise. She used the word *sex* as a target word.

SEX

Lust.
Disgust.
Sick.
Yucky.
Warm.
Dirty.

In looking over the list she initially reported feeling embarrassed that many of the words were negative in tone, and she wanted to add others that were more positive. I clarified that the first list was probably a clearer representation of how the child/teenager felt, and suggested she go ahead and create a second list, bearing in mind that the second list would be the work of her adult self. The completed list looked like this:

SEX

Child/Teen	Adult
Lust.	Fun.
Disgust.	Connecting.
Sick.	Pleasure.
Yucky.	Caring.
Warm.	Touch.
Dirty.	Celebration.

RELEASING & REPLACING

In doing this work, this client was able to see how she sometimes felt conflicted about sex. Often, her body felt willing but her mind was defensively guarded. At times the adult part of herself controlled her sex life, at times the child controlled it, and at other times they conflicted. In working on the issue, she was able to see that the child self essentially saw sexuality as an unnatural body function, and paired this with her memory of the teaching that the body is the "temple of the Holy Spirit", and would be defiled if used for any other purpose. We also looked together at the teachings regarding the sixth Commandment, taken from the an old Baltimore Catechism, which reads:

"What does the sixth Commandment forbid? The sixth Commandment forbids all impurity and immodesty in words, looks, and actions, whether alone or with others. Examples of this would be: touching one's own body or that of another without necessity simply to satisfy sinful curiosity, impure conversations, dirty jokes, looking at bad pictures, undue familiarity with the opposite sex".

In healing her sexual self, she developed a plan for enhancing and developing her natural, healthy sexuality. Her initial plan read as follows:

SEXUAL HEALING PLAN

1) Put the adult self in charge of the child self.
2) Have the adult re-educate the child regarding her body:
   a) Teach her that sexuality is wonderful.
   b) Teach her that her genitals are there to be enjoyed.
   c) Teach her that lustiness is good and that the adult self will decide how and when to let this power out, safely and responsibly.

d) Show the child/teenager what her genitals look like, using a mirror.

e) Help the child let go of fears relating to touching the genitals. Emphasize this as a private, personal and delightful activity.

As her work progressed, she re-evaluated her initial plan, adding on new items as she saw fit. As with other healing work, it is important to create a framework that is designed to suit your own needs.

Another technique is to sit down and write a list of sexual activities you have never enjoyed but at times have been tempted to do. Keep in mind that the Church taught us that temptation came from the Devil, a sinister and scary figure to many young children. Even though you may no longer believe in the Devil, the "aura" associated with sexual thoughts, ideas and practices that are not strictly conventional may feel sinister or give you feelings of discomfort at the very least. One client said she had always wanted to play a specific sexual game with her husband but had felt too guilty and "creepy" to do so, despite the fact that the game in question did not seem bizarre or harmful to her. She decided to allow herself to be open to the possibility of playing it when the right opportunity presented itself.

Once you have developed your list, ask yourself the following question: Why haven't I done this activity? If the answer is related to the fact that it would be physically or emotionally harmful to the self or others, accept this at face value: a determination made by the adult self to protect you and your partner from bodily harm, and to ensure a loving connection is maintained. If the answer suggests that sex is dirty, too much fun, too lustful, or too wild, ask if this is an expression of the inner child's fear of breaking out of sexual taboos learned at home, at school, or at Church. If so, it is time for the adult to take over and begin to allow you to experience some of the pleasure, closeness, and desire you have denied yourself to this point. In order to do this, you may want to begin to identify with other adults whom you see as presently engaged in rich, vibrant sexual lives. Avoidance of all talk about meaningful sexuality keeps our society guilt-ridden. Women's magazines may be helpful in providing useful information about couples' sexuality but they rarely provide ideas for breaking through the "silence barrier". When was the last time you heard two couples talking about how their love for one another is increasing through their sexuality? The assumption that many of us make is that talking about sex involves spelling out every detail of lovemaking. This may be the *content* of a sexual encounter. It is not the *process*, however, and we could all benefit by learning about one another's growth in this area.

Many people that I have worked with have had significant breakthroughs by talking about sex, and by hearing themselves talk about it. Another means of working on sexual issues is to imagine yourself as a teacher of a class on sexuality. Consider what your teaching plan would look like. Practice looking into a mirror and work on developing a comfort level in talking about sex. This may take time, and may need to be used in addition to other methods, but over time it will have an effect. Here is an example, provided by a survey respondent who is a social worker:

> "I have just recently left the Church and this comes at a time when I've been doing a lot of reviewing in my spiritual life, looking at how my old behaviors, trained into me by the Church, don't fit with who I am today. I'm 29.
>
> "The Church says masturbation is wrong, sex before marriage is wrong, getting married without the intention of having a baby is wrong, homosexual behavior is wrong. I thought—isn't this interesting! God gave us these bodies, but we're not supposed to touch them, not supposed to look

at them or enjoy them, and it doesn't make sense! When I masturbate, I have all of these things playing in my head—'this is wrong, you're not supposed to do this', yet as a social worker working with kids I can talk to them about it, teaching them what is appropriate sexually and what's not. It feels right for *them* but still doesn't feel right for *me*. (I've gotten rid of the idea that sex is just for having babies, though, because I've finished having my family, and now I have sex *just for fun!*)"

[Note: I have realized that I have never been clear as to exactly what is—or was—the Church's position on the validity of sexual behavior within a marriage once the wife is beyond child-bearing years. *Is it allowed??*]

This recovering Catholic continues to have struggles with some areas of her sexual life, but it is clear that she has begun to learn what she herself is teaching others. I am not suggesting you go out and round up a group of students as a learning tool, but once you begin to feel competent at talking to yourself about your beliefs, it can be useful to try out your ideas on a willing partner or friend: not merely with the intention of receiving feedback, but in order to practice hearing yourself speak, and, in order to allow the *world* (as represented by your partner), to hear that you are changing and allowing yourself to adopt newer beliefs, ones that more accurately reflect your present day self.

Another way of increasing your comfort level regarding sexuality is to consider working with a sex therapist on the issues that cause the most concern. Unlike psychotherapists, who may deal with a number of different life problems, sex therapists generally focus specifically on sexual functioning. Simply allowing yourself to acknowledge your sexuality in this way can be a powerful healing tool as, again, there are few places in society where sex is discussed in an open and accepting way. A recovering Catholic who has clearly done a lot of thinking on this issue wrote the following:

> "To me, sexuality is the most poignant and powerful representation of the joy of being on earth. It is a celebration of my alive-ness. The problem is that it can be so wonderful, fun, and exciting that I'm aware again of feeling *too good*. Most of us Catholics have been programmed to believe that feeling too good is *bad*. And *that's* too bad."

We feel like Adam and Eve, frolicking around in the garden, having a great time, and then suddenly we remember, either consciously or on some deeper level, that we screwed up somehow, and the sexual problems that are individual for us begin to take over. It is unfortunate that we have wasted so much time feeling guilty, fallen, and led into temptation. It is time to move on, into a satisfying and healthy appreciation of our love and desire.

CHAPTER NINE
PARENT WORK

*A*nother way to work on Catholic issues is to talk them through with one's parents. Of course this avenue is not open to everyone; but if you are fortunate enough to have a parent or parents who are capable of discussing the past with relative open-mindedness, then this can truly represent an invaluable source of insight for you, and at the same time offer a great opportunity to enrich your relationship with them. A word of caution: some of these open-minded parents may be more than willing to sit with you and listen, and support your growth process—but they may *still* go into a sort of Catholic "denial" about some of the events. For example, I see my own mother—a practicing Catholic—as being someone who has offered me many hours of patient support in recent years as I have struggled to make sense of the past. She has never attempted to sway me or lure me back into the fold; and in fact she herself has been questioning many of the rigid teachings of the Church. Despite this broad-mindedness, there are times when her denial kicks in.

While writing this book, I talked to her about the results of some of my interviews. I told her about a recent interview in which a former Catholic described having been sexually abused by a parish priest as a teenager, while in a swimming pool. My mother said she found that hard to believe, saying "They would have been supervised. Someone would have seen it." The problem here is that there has been such an effective and systematic idealization of the clergy: it is simply very hard for many people to believe that priests and nuns could have abused children. It is particularly difficult for Catholics to believe, having been raised to see priests and nuns as "next to God"; but the fact remains that abuse *did* happen, and it needs to be recognized as such—not in order to seek revenge, but with the intention of coming out of the cloud of denial that surrounds us.

There may be other roadblocks too. Some parents may simply be too fearful to hear what you have to say. They may have lived their lives locked into the tenets and mores of their faith; and this absolute adherence to the Church's authority may in some ways have become necessary to their psychological survival. Many respondents to the questionnaire both implicitly and explicitly stated that they felt disconnected from their parents on issues related to Catholicism, and cited past family arguments or avoidance of conflict as their main reasons for continued unwillingness to express their thoughts and feelings. For them, "let sleeping dogs lie" is the operating principle. One woman said she begins to have old feelings of fear and shame rise up whenever she visits her mother on the West coast, knowing that her mother will invariably make mention of her local pastor, Church functions, and Church happenings, all in a thinly disguised attempt to reintroduce her to Catholicism. These feelings of disconnectedness and guilt can interfere with creating a rewarding experience between parent and adult child. This is an example of the problems that arise whenever either the parent or the adult child decides that the only acceptable outcome in any conversation is to *convert* the other person to his or her side. This just represents more black and white thinking, with the pain and turmoil that inevitably goes along with that, all of which is unnecessary and can be avoided by changing the *motive* behind the discussion, at least on your part: if the desire is to *share* yourself, rather than to convert the enemy, then the whole encounter takes on a different shape.

Despite possible discomfort, talking with parents can be of great value, particularly when these same parents have been generally supportive of you in other areas of life—regarding your own family or work issues, for example. If this is the case, it would be reasonable to assume that they may also be ready to hear your thoughts and concerns regarding having grown up Catholic. In contrast, those parents who have had a difficult time in general accepting their children's need for individuation will also be less available today. All of this is by way of saying that the first step in considering Parent Work is to make a careful evaluation, in as objective a way as possible, of what may be realistic.

The benefit of working with a group or a therapist in this process is invaluable if you find yourself uncertain of how or whether to proceed. If you decide to talk to your parents, your primary purpose must be clear from the start. If the purpose is to dump a lot of guilt onto your parents, you are likely to meet with intense resistance, which will be demonstrated in their characteristic style. This may involve, for instance, a sudden change of subject, angry attacking, passive-aggressive comments you can't defend, silence, coldness, or a tendency to treat you as a child, to name a few. Sometimes, an *un*characteristic response is a sign of a breakthrough in general communications. If, for example, your mother suddenly became very angry hearing your stories and experiences, and this was an unusual reaction for her, you might also be moved to respond in an unusual way, possibly clearing up some old mis-understandings and resentments. Ordinarily, however, dumping guilt only tends to stir defensive tendencies in others, including our parents, and they will likely respond in a way that will not be useful, creating renewed guilt and anger in you. This is not to say that clearing out anger along the way is not entirely appropriate. Having a good sounding board in the form of a group, friend, or therapist is essential. The main purpose, however, needs to be to help them get to know who you *were* and who you *are* as a recovering Catholic, so as to deepen the relationship between you, and so as to free up your inner child so that you can become more creative and self-propelled. This may involve more than a one-shot conversation, and may be an ongoing process; it will depend on your own intuition about how far to progress.

If you decide to speak to your parent(s), consider several general guidelines before starting:

1) Be aware of your purpose. Is it to change your parents views in any way? You will need to be unflinchingly honest with your-self about this. The tendency to deny your desire to change them may be great, and you may have a secret agenda. You might want to consider what the secret agenda could be, *if* you had one, as a means of routing it out. Changing your parents' views is not a useful motive, in that it is an attempt to control. As recovering Catholics, we are looking for opportunities to let go of the need to control others, a tendency we may have learned through the Church and through our parents. Is your purpose to shame your parents? Again, many of us experienced deep feelings of shame, particularly in the Catholic educational system, and have learned to shame others as a result. We need to remember that this is no more useful for others than it was for us. Other possible motives might be to hear an apology or

to engage in conflict. If you are able to identify any of these, congratulate yourself for your honesty, and clear the motive out before moving on.

2) Sit down and write out what you want your parent(s) to know. Get as clear as possible. Be sensitive to potential resistance they may feel. Allow this awareness to color the words you use, but not the meaning behind them. While it is important for you to express yourself clearly, you know what kinds of language, gestures, and facial expressions are going to set the stage for the atmospheric scene you want to create. This is neither manipulation nor "co-dependency" but a common-sense, open-eyed approach to the situation. Also be sensitive to exactly how much you want to share and give yourself permission to share only what you wish, without *guilt* entering in and telling you that you have to tell *everything*, just like you did in the confessional.

3) Prepare yourself and your parent by asking, *before* any sit-down session, if they could do you a favor and follow a few guidelines, as a way of helping you. These are designed to give a sense of freedom, as this may be an anxiety-provoking situation for you. Hearing your parents agree to the "conditions" may relieve a substantial amount of this anxiety, and give you added confidence. Examples of guidelines might include those listed below, but it would be the most helpful for you to choose your own, based on who you are, and what your own personal needs are. Many of my clients have been shocked to see how readily their parents went along with the conditions, and have gone on to use the same basic idea in other areas, and with other people, including siblings, former teachers, and clergy.

GUIDELINES FOR A PARENT SESSION

1) I would like to talk to you for ___ minutes without interruption.

2) I would like you to indicate that you're understanding me (be specific and descriptive regarding how).

3) I'd appreciate your looking at me/looking away from me when I talk.

4) I don't want you to give your opinion. *Or*
   I want you to give your opinion at the end. *Or*
   I want to hear what you think, but not today.

5) I don't want you to tell me I'm not remembering it right.

6) I don't want you to compare your childhood with mine.

7) I don't want you to defend the Church, Sister ____, Father _____.

8) I want to be able to show feelings without you showing feelings too. *Or*
   I want us both to feel free to share our feelings.

Whether to approach your parents in this work is an individual decision. Again, we are getting away from the idea that there is one right way and one wrong way. The decision about how and when to proceed is also individual. The nature of your relationship with your parent(s), the amount of contact with him or her in childhood, the extent of their involvement with Catholicism presently and in the past: these may all be factors that effect your choice. Some clients are vehement in their reaction to even the suggestion of doing this exercise. If your immediate response is "no *way*", accept that, as a means of protecting yourself. It would still be helpful to stop and look at why you feel that way, and what your fears are. The desire to do it eventually may or may not surface, or you may find a different way to achieve the same purpose. One survey respondent who said she would never think of approaching her parents, told this story:

"I was raised with the unshakable belief that marriage was a sacrament, and as such was only valid if undergone with a Catholic, in a Catholic Church. I managed to remain unscathed by the popular Catholic belief that anyone not baptized a Catholic would never see heaven. It just never made sense to me in light of a loving and forgiving God. As I matured, I found myself moving farther and farther from the Church, for a variety of reasons, until I was sure I had broken all ties. The indelible quality of that mark on the soul became apparent when I decided to marry. My parents were curious about this guy with whom I was hanging around. The limits of their curiosity, however, extended no farther than these three, most crucial questions. Is he Catholic? Has he always been single? Is he white? Anyone incapable of answering yes to all three was automatically unsuitable and it was expected that I would come to my senses and find a more appropriate candidate with whom to share the sacrament of marriage. It became apparent that he had brainwashed me with pagan heresy, illicit sex and drugs, because instead of dropping him like the hot potato from hell that he was, I moved in with him. My mother tried to hit me when I told her, then cried because I was using birth control and made me promise I would not tell my father for fear that it would kill him. She immediately disowned me.

"This Catholic cold war went on for two years. During that time, I never heard from my father, which bothered me little and had no effect on my life. Eventually, M. and I decided to get married after about a year of living in sin. In my innocence, I believed that were we to marry in the Church, my parents would come around. We went to the priest at my old parish, having agreed to be truthful but to offer no information unless specifically asked. The very first question on the form damned us—the address. When the priest saw we shared an address, he said we had a problem. If we lived together in haste it was his belief that we would divorce in haste and he would not marry us. I cried, Bob steamed, but the icing on the cake was this bit of advice. He told us to leave his office and walk across the hall to the pastor—we could lie to him because 'he'd marry anyone'. I wasn't clear about which part of this bothered me more—the rejection, or the humiliation of the duplicity. This was Bob's introduction to Catholicism, by the way, and he was disgusted. We eventually found a priest who would marry us without the need to lie, and had a beautiful wedding which my parents refused to attend.

"My parents eventually warmed up to us after we had children. They are still heartbroken that our children aren't baptized. My mother prays for me all the time, and they are convinced that I'll eventually come around to their way of thinking. They wouldn't be able to listen to my opinions, and anything that deviates from the Catholic norm they consider heresy. This would be a problem, because these days I find myself in diametric opposition to almost everything the Church says and does. I completely disagree with its stand on birth control, homosexuality, war and violence, male and female roles, etc., etc. From my mother's side, she is terrified that my children aren't baptized and will go to Limbo. My children do not spend time with their grandparents because of the logistics involved, but were they closer, this issue of religion would become a major battlefield."

VISUALIZATION

In the situation outlined above, direct parent work is impossible, and in order to preserve the valuable elements that already exist in the relationship, her goals might best be accomplished by working alone. However, even though direct work may be ruled out, there is no reason why you cannot achieve significant benefits by doing visualization work. You can *imagine* your parents responding to you in a way that meets your needs through playing out this scene in your mind, using the guidelines discussed above. In this way you are able to feel what it would be like if you were *both* able to break through fear and doubt. The effect of this exercise can be powerful, because you can have your parents say things that *feel* true to you, despite the fact that they may not in reality be able to say them.

Visualization is best facilitated by closing your eyes, with feet resting flat on the floor, and your body in a comfortable position. Take time to get into a feeling of restfulness. If you want to listen to a relaxation tape, quiet music, or other possibly familiar mode of relaxing, do this. Avoid mood-altering substances while doing this work, however. Keep in mind that you have the option to move at whatever rate is comfortable to you. You can start off slowly and tentatively or more quickly, as you desire. If you encounter resistance in yourself or your parent you have the option to think things through and decide how to manage this before moving on. Remember that both you and your parents were taught that there are correct and incorrect ways of looking at life processes as put forward by the Church. Both you and your parent may be inclined towards rigidity and both of you may experience fear of rocking the boat or saying something "sacrilegious" as a result. Keep in mind that it is okay to be messy and disorganized, and that your movement forward will aid you. Also remember that your purpose is not to convince or be convinced, but simply to share your life in a way that feels meaningful to you.

Here is an example of an initial conversation between a mother and daughter using visualization:

Daughter: "Mom, I want you to understand something about why I left the Church since we've never really talked about this in an open way. There are certain things I'd like you to do."

(If it's hard for you to imagine your mother respecting your thoughts, do it first with your mom acting in her typical way and you acting in *your* typical way—be loud, silent, change the subject; essentially follow your typical pattern of interaction from the past. The purpose in this is to "get it out of your system." Then proceed.)

Mom: "This feels frightening to me. I'm afraid you are going to put down *my* beliefs in the process. I'm still a Catholic, you know. I'm also concerned that something will be said that could hurt us both, based on some of what has happened in the past."

Daughter: "I'll talk only about my own feelings and ideas, not about your beliefs, but one of the things I want is for you to simply allow me to *have* my own thoughts, knowing that we're different but still care for each other. The other thing that I want is for you to listen without shaking your head back and forth, as if to say 'No.' You are very expressive with your body, and I'm afraid I will get confused if I start seeing a 'No'. Would you do these things for me?"

Mother: "Yes."

Daughter: "Can I tell you if I'm not feeling good about what is going on?"

Mother: "Yes."

Some of my clients have a good laugh when I seriously suggest visualization work, and take a cynical view of the whole idea. They have spent so many years holding on to simmering resentment about how their parents handled certain events, that the concept of receiving what they need (even through visualization) brings with it feelings of incredulity or anger. And yet this work can sometimes be the most beneficial to those who have the hardest time contemplating it.

Visualization can also be useful as a *preparatory* tool before an actual meeting with a parent. First, imagine an uncensored, unprepared conversation with your parents. In doing so, you can get clearer about how you might ordinarily sabotage your efforts, unintentionally, resulting in further tension, conflict and guilt rather than movement. Imagine yourself taking risks that you might not ordinarily take, experimenting with speaking in a different tone of voice, or using language that is unfamiliar to you. Doing this work will help you feel more confident about the live scene between you and your parent, and assist you in anticipating his or her reactions at certain points, followed by your way of dealing with these reactions.

Another option is to role-play, with another person taking the part of your parent. Your partner in this exercise should be given as much information as possible about your parent's stance regarding the Church, including catch-phrases he or she uses, and specific beliefs and areas to emphasize. It is useful if the other person is also a present or former Catholic, as this will obviously cut out the necessity for a lot of explanation. (On the other hand, I have worked with clients whose spouses were non-Catholics and whose lack of personal emotional involvement made the role-plays easier to do). Exchanging roles at some point can also be helpful as a means of developing some compassion and understanding about your parent's struggle with your current beliefs.

For those of you who decide to work with your parents directly, a payoff of sorts is waiting at the conclusion of the work *regardless* of whether or not it goes well. The payoff is this: either you will discover that your parent has heard your experiences, as simple or as complex as they might be, *or* you will discover, up front, that they are *unable* to witness your experience, and may, in fact, be in a lot of denial about what life was like for you. Despite the possible pain inherent in that realization, there is also something purifying and freeing in the understanding that your parent simply can't support the inner child in a meaningful way on this issue. This can ultimately be a relief, for both of you, allowing other options to reveal themselves.

Adults whose parents have died can also do this work, either through visualization or role-play. The initial preparatory work is the same, as you clarify your purpose and decide how you want your parent to be. Many adult children experience very profound connections with their parent in this process.

CHAPTER TEN

PSYCHOTHERAPY AND OTHER TOOLS

PSYCHOTHERAPY

*C*ounseling can be an effective way of sorting out what you were taught as a child, and allowing your self to retain or discard these beliefs. For some, this may be a relatively short process. I have found this to be true particularly for people raised in the later decades of this century, as well as for those who attended public rather than parochial schools and who therefore received less formal religious training. Others need more time simply because of who they are, or because they are carrying more toxic baggage; for example, situations in which a person experienced physical or sexual abuse by a member of the clergy are unlikely to be resolved in a few weeks. Again, one purpose of working through issues involving clergy, parents, and others in authority is to recognize the fact that those who hurt you were human and subject to human error. They were not representatives of God in the sense that they had permission to violate others. Although the adult in you might agree, it is likely that the child part has held on to the original teaching, and so has continued to feel guilty and responsible.

Finding a therapist for this purpose may initially be a difficult process; conventional psychotherapy has traditionally limited itself to dealing with psychological issues, while spiritual counselors typically operate from within the framework of a particular Church or religious group. Many psychologists and other mental health professionals may feel unprepared to deal with spiritual issues. Likewise, many spiritual counselors feel ill-prepared to deal with psychological issues, and are often open in saying so. Also, many recovering Catholics may have strong feelings about seeing a therapist who deals with spiritual issues, as these same people are generally supportive of a specific Christian sect. Those therapists willing to include a focus on spirituality may not have examined their own spiritual issues, or conversely they may have rigid and dogmatic religious beliefs. The purpose in bringing all of this to the foreground is not to discourage you, but to clarify that, as a thoughtful adult, you now have the power to pick and choose people to help you. It is my impression that there has been an increase over the past ten years or so in the number of qualified therapists who can handle this combination of emotional, psychological and spiritual conflict that confront so many recovering Catholics. A therapist needs to be hired in the same way you might hire someone to care for your children or an elderly parent. What are his or her credentials? Have they worked with both spiritual and psychological issues in the past? Have they worked on their own spiritual issues and are they willing to share parts of their own experience when appropriate? Ask if they have a particular approach to the work and ask what kinds of techniques they have used with others. The idea here is not to know every aspect of the way the therapist works, but to get a gist of their way of working and thinking, and whether you can feel comfortable with that person. A new client reported to me, for example, that she had approached a therapist to gain help with a particular spiritual problem that had emotional and physical repercussions. She asked the therapist a bit about how he worked. Although he was very candid, and appeared knowledgeable and competent, she felt by his manner that they would not work well together, as she wanted a therapist with more warmth. She gave herself permission to move on and find a therapist she would able to work with.

In terms of techniques and approaches to the work, keep in mind that any technique is used to its greatest advantage when it is tailor-made to suit a particular individual. At the same time, some therapists tend to focus more on verbal approaches aimed at achieving cognitive change while others center on action-oriented work. Still others tend to work predominantly with feelings. I have found that the most creative and lasting change comes with an emphasis on thought, feeling *and* action. Although it may be tempting for both client and counselor (particularly if both were raised as Catholics) to make shorthand assumptions about Catholic-based experience, many factors influence and alter personal life, making it unique for each of us. One type of Catholic teaching, going to hell for consciously eating meat on Friday, for example, may have created a strong emotional response in one person and virtually none in another. It is important, therefore, to speak up if a counselor appears to be interpreting your words in a way that seem scrambled by his or her own experience.

Another alternative is to see a therapist raised in another faith or raised without a religious background. The advantage to this is the additional capacity for objectivity on the therapist's part. The disadvantage is a possible feeling of being misunderstood or feeling that the counselor hasn't "been there". Also, some time needs to be taken in order to explain various beliefs of the Catholic Church. Some Catholics clients report receiving blank stares, questioning or incredulous looks, when talking about Catholic issues with non-Catholics. It is important that a counselor is able to validate all of your experience, while being aware of your desire to change some of your thinking in relation to it. It is also important for the client to take the lead in deciding if and when to join a religion, religious group, or make any other type of spiritual affiliation. Many of us grew up having to accept a multitude of religious beliefs without question. We now have the choice to decide for ourselves. A client shared this experience with me:

> "Several years ago I worked with a very New Age spiritual counselor, and I expressed considerable feeling, allowing myself to open up some fears related to having grown up Catholic. At the end of the session I told her I had explored several avenues since my early 20's and had been attending an Episcopal Church for a while. She said: 'Church?! You don't need to be going to any Church at all! Everything you need is inside of you!' While I agreed in part with what she was saying, the *experience* as I listened to her words was one of being admonished and lectured to, and the rigidity of her position ironically reenacted my childhood experience in the Catholic Church: her *liberal* dogmatism was no more useful to me than the conservative dogmatism of the Church. Her remark was off-base in another way too: it didn't respect my need at the time to be a part of a spiritual community."

One valuable aspect of therapy, and other interactional work, is that it allows you to have your confusion, pain, anger, and other feelings *witnessed* by others. The thought of doing this may seem alien to the child part of many recovering Catholics because it is such a different experience from that of early childhood, when individual needs were seen as invalid or unimportant. Ironically, the Church *did* offer a place, in the form of the confessional, where we could reveal our private difficulties; but this was a dark, secretive and guilty place. Many of the questionnaire respondents reported that they alternately used the confessional as a dumping ground for behaviors they felt guilty about (but intended to continue), or they simply made up sins to confess. They reported the priest's response as often "bland", "uninvolved", "curious", or "disgusted". Few respondents indicated that they had felt connected to or cared for by the priest and many had felt frightened as little children. It is therefore especially important for recovering Catholics to work with a counselor who provides a clearly open, accepting, caring framework. A feeling of safety is especially important for those Catholics who were physically or sexually abused by adults in the Church. The feeling of vulnerability inherent in discussing these issues can be great, and requires great trust to match it.

GROUP WORK

Working with a trained therapist in a group is another way to have feelings witnessed and experienced in an open but protected setting. Group members will undoubtedly share many similar understandings, which become a starting point for developing connections with others. In a group setting that is specifically for recovering Catholics it is critical for the therapist to have been a practicing Catholic. A therapist who has never had the experience of being Catholic would have understandable difficulty in relating to the *culture* of Catholicism, an essential ingredient for group work, as many cultural issues will emerge over the course of the work.

Some people may elect to form a "leaderless" group to go through the treatment process. My concern here is that often feelings come to the surface which may be overwhelming to the individual, and the group may not always be equipped to support that person and help him move through the process. If the group is unable to contain the individual's emerging feelings, or if all the members are identifying with them with equal intensity, the group itself may have trouble reaching the resolution stage, and will often end up disbanding as a result. This will almost certainly lead to an increased sense of failure and hopelessness. For this reason it can be invaluable to work with a trained therapist who has identified and worked through some of his or her own struggles related to Catholicism, and who has sufficient experience in group work to help the group as a whole move through difficult stages successfully. Notice I refer to having moved through *some* of his or her own struggles related to Catholicism. A therapist who is unable to talk about his or her own growth, when appropriate, will inadvertently encourage the group to adopt the old good/bad, right/wrong, heaven/hell polarizations that got us all in trouble in the first place.

ROLE-PLAYING

Role-playing typically involves two or more people. The role-play can be spontaneous or it can be "scripted", with each individual saying his or her lines. One client scripted a very effective role-play surrounding an event in grade school in which he had felt deeply humiliated by one of his teachers. In the script he essentially repeated the earlier scenario, while his wife played the role of the nun. They read off their lines, allowing him to get in touch with a multitude of feelings in his child-self: humiliation, anger, fear and sadness. As an *adult*, he was also able to feel power, compassion, safety and exhilaration. He then wrote a second script, in which he integrated his adult self with the child; and using this integrated self he openly and confidently told the nun how he was feeling, in a way that would not have been tolerated in the original situation, of course. In this second script he also had the sister apologize; and he allowed himself to feel a sense of compassion and forgiveness. Although this was a serious piece of work, he and his wife also enjoyed a lot of laughter, which can be a great release if it is *one* element of the process, and not an avoidance of feelings of pain and guilt.

PSYCHODRAMA

Psychodrama is similar to role-playing, in that individuals take on specific roles, although it is a more expansive tool, in the sense that a *group* of people can work together, assuming different roles or exchanging them as needed. Psychodrama can also incorporate props; and it generally involves greater use of the body. Using the previous example, for instance, opportunities for recognizing the possible feelings of the nun, my client, and other children in the classroom could be explored using desks, chairs, a pointer and so on, for props. Generally speaking, psychodrama is best used in a supervised setting with an experienced leader. Since it is spontaneous and often involves intense emotions rising to the surface, a "safety net" is important.

Working with others can be an invaluable way of moving through old feelings of loss, sadness, guilt and pain, because it allows us to finally *join* and *support* one another, something we were often unable to do in childhood during the course of frightening, confusing, or humiliating events. As children, we had no power over the adults who educated us, nor did we have power over our parents. Working in a group provides a forum for regaining a sense of safety and power through interaction. It also allows us to recognize the numerous ways in which our feelings, which we may have thought of as unique, were and are shared by many others; thus through connection with one another, we are provided a way out of our isolation.

LETTER WRITING

Letter writing is another means for us to clarify our thoughts and feelings about our Catholic upbringing. The purpose behind letter writing is to isolate a particular Catholic person or group (for example a nun, a priest, the Pope, a parent, or a C.C.D. group) and to tell that person or group through a letter how you feel about the way in which you were treated or what you were taught as a child. In a sense, you are acting on behalf of the Catholic kid in you, speaking up for him or her in a way that was not possible in childhood. You may choose to send your letter, or you may use it strictly for your own healing work. At first it is useful to simply let all of your thoughts and feelings hang out. This means avoiding the urge to censor what you have to say. This can be difficult for many Catholics, as our tendency is to assume that our own personal thoughts and beliefs are secondary to those expounded by the Church—or by whatever authority may have replaced it. Even though your adult self may no longer hold these beliefs, the child self was taught not to question the authority of the Church in matters of morals and doctrine, and the concepts of sin and punishment were commonly used as deterrents. Another obstacle to letting feelings and ideas come to the surface is that in doing so, we usually create a *mess*. Our Catholic upbringing taught us there is never a need for a mess. We were taught there were a set of appropriate reactions to every difficult situation. We were not encouraged to be disorganized, we were encouraged to find the perfect way to do God's will as specified by the Catholic Church. Now, we need to give ourselves permission to be Picasso paintings, allowing things to feel disjointed temporarily as we work to release the past and move on. We also need to see this as a positive, growthful process, with the emphasis on what is changing, rather than on what remains incomplete in our development. It is for these reasons that it is important for your *adult* self to write any letters you choose to compose, as it is the child who is in need of healing and support.

Before writing, have a conference with your inner child. Sit down, close your eyes, and tell the child what you are going to do. Listen for a response. If you meet up with a great deal of resistance (which could come in the form of anger, balking, daydreaming, or anxiety, among others) your first job is to deal with that resistance before moving on to the letter-writing itself. The child was forced to believe many things and to do many things; he or she had little personal power in decision-making when it came to spiritual matters, and may have been generally disrespected at home. Thoughts, questions, and creative ideas may have rarely, if ever, been tapped. If the child resists the idea of doing a letter, accept that as a legitimate feeling. This doesn't mean that you won't go on to write at a later date; it simply means you are allowing time to express his or her fear openly before moving on. It is through addressing these feelings that opportunities for healing arise, because usually these feelings will be highly specific, pointing to the areas that posed the greatest amount of difficulty.

Here is a description of this process, written by one of my clients:

"When I decided to compose letters (to a grade school nun and the Pope, respectively) it took me several weeks to actually write them. Initially, I felt mentally stuck: there seemed to be a lot to say, but my confusion as to how to say it dominated the situation. Although it seemed ridiculous, my kid self felt terrified at the thought of writing anything in an angry or blaming way. She told me that if the Pope got that letter he would be really, really mad at me, and the priests in the Vatican would find a way of making sure I got punished even though I wasn't a practicing Catholic any longer. She also said nobody could say anything about the Pope that wasn't nice because the Pope was almost exactly like God and God would get mad, too. I just listened to her and acted as a Mom. I reassured her that the Pope couldn't hurt her, that he was an ordinary man who used to go camping in the woods in Poland, that I didn't believe God ever got mad at anyone the way humans do, and that anyway we didn't have to mail the letter if we didn't want to.

In working on the letter to Sister J., I focused on trying to express anger at the strict way she disciplined, like the times when she forced our class to sit for a half hour with our hands behind our backs whenever one kid misbehaved. I told my kid part that I would be talking to Sister J. as one grownup to another. Over a period of weeks, I experienced a softening, a yielding in the child part of myself, with an ultimate willingness on her part for me to write the letters. Eventually, she herself contributed much of the content information which made up the letters."

Some of you may be capable of writing letters on the spot. Make sure the child has been consulted, so that you are integrated in your approach to the work. Also, be particularly sensitive to the child's fear of bodily harm emanating from writing to an influential adult from the past: if you were one of those who experienced physical or sexual abuse as a child, this will most likely still be a live issue for you.

The decision about whether to mail the letter is a personal one. Usually, the decision is made as the letter progresses. A letter you decide to send may need to be amended in order to make it acceptable to the adult part of yourself. If the letter is highly blaming in tone, the adult self may want to use it for your private use only. In my client's case, she chose not to edit the letter, and not to send it either. I suggested she might want to burn it in a ceremonial way to signify her willingness to let go of all of the anger, fear and blame carried through the years. She liked the idea and followed through with it. Other possibilities may occur to you as you move forward.

One caution: if the letter is blaming and venomous and you don't edit it, find a way to release it rather than hold onto it for an extended period of time. While it might be useful to temporarily live with a letter that spells out old feelings clearly, it is unhealthy to sit in it indefinitely. Be willing to let go of the emotional baggage connected with the unpleasant experiences. Ideas will then surface as to how to go about doing so. The ultimate purpose of this and all healing work is to feel a sense of inner calm and quiet. If you are working alone exclusively and find that your feelings are becoming overwhelming, give yourself permission to find a spiritual advisor, a willing therapist, or other caring person to work it through with you. You can be specific with this person about where you are in the process and what you want from them, while still feeling confused. Again, it is possible to feel fearful and uncertain and still to be in charge.

Letter writing can be most helpful for those of us who like to write and are comfortable expressing ourselves in this way. If writing itself is an uncomfortable chore for you, you could use a tape recorder and dictate your thoughts and feelings in this way.

Here is an example of part of a letter written to a former teacher:

Dear Brother Anthony,

I am writing to tell you some of my feelings about what went on in fourth grade. I'm doing so in order that I can move on with my life. You see, you *really* messed me up, and I have a lot of anger and hatred toward you that needs to get out. What the hell were you thinking of? Did you *really* think that you were teaching me valuable lessons when you bullied and humiliated me in front of the other boys? What sort of power trip were you on? I'll never forget the time you made me slap my own hand till my wrist turned red, in front of the whole class, for something so trivial I can't even remember what it was, probably talking out loud.

It seems as I look back that you must have been getting some twisted sadistic (sexual?) satisfaction out of this, and yet you pretended it was for some bullshit purpose to do with saving my soul and making me clean for God. I can't believe that *you* really accepted that. I used to long for terrible accidents to happen to you, and then I'd get so guilty for having bad thoughts and being so sick. But it was *you* who was sick, and perverted and twisted, and you never should have been allowed to be around impressionable young children; you should have been being rehabilitated somewhere for your poisoned mind. I feel you owe me—and all the other boys— a huge apology for the incredible hurt you afflicted. I would never allow a child of mine to come anywhere near you. You taught me nothing, except how to belittle myself. At least I've gotten to a point where I'm able to see this clearly and begin to get it out of my system—I just hope that you are no longer screwing kids up in the name of Catholicism.

It needs to be stressed that this particular exercise is not an end in and of itself, and it would be clearly harmful to get stuck in such a blaming attitude; and yet identifying and being honest with your true feelings is a very necessary part of the process, as a means to move beyond the stagnation and constraint that comes with unexpressed and unarticulated anger. The goal is to feel the anger *and* to release it. Sometimes, simply expressing the anger brings with it a sense of release. At other times, it can be very freeing to imagine the person you are writing to responding in a healing way:

> "I closed my eyes and imagined Brother Anthony talking to me about the letter. I imagined him answering my concerns in a really thoughtful way. It was amazing, really, because he looked the way he would have looked if he had been able to be caring back then. The words he used were distinctive and had his own flavor about them. I imagined him really acknowledging my concerns, and I felt finally understood. I just cried and cried. I realized at the same time that whatever guilt I had been holding on to for the 'offenses' in my childhood contact with him was simply gone".

Letter writing is a healing tool that may feel useful. If you don't enjoy writing, other ways of working may be more helpful to you. If you decide to work with letter writing, give yourself permission to make decisions slowly about how to proceed. If you decide to send your letter(s), take time to anticipate possible reactions and think about how you might respond, both to yourself and to the younger parts of yourself.

MEDITATION

Meditation is a way of getting in touch with the deepest and most potent part of your own being. Some people may refer to that part as God, or use some label; others may think of it simply as a relaxed state of mind. Conventional Christian religions tend to use the term 'God' exclusively to define this power. I don't think the name is as important as the recognition that when we get quiet and centered it is easier to get ideas about how to best live our lives.

Meditation is often associated with spirituality and can have a bad reputation with former Catholics, who may connect it with long and often boring periods during the old Latin Mass, when we were supposed to be meditating on Christ's love for us. Our thoughts then may have trailed off into musings about what to do after Mass, or we may have fastened our attention onto mundane details concerning the hat of the woman in front of us or the man in the next pew. There are certainly a group of Catholics who strongly identified with the mystical beauty of the old Mass, but little guidance or instruction was generally given about how to enter a meditative state, and so the feeling of real connection between ourselves and the deeper part within was not experienced by many of us. And to make matters worse, there was often the added reminder that our inability to truly enter a meditative state was just one more example of our spiritual inferiority and inadequacy.

One of the benefits of meditation is the feeling of freedom that it can bring. The thoughts, feelings and experiences that come up during a period of meditation are your own, arising from a deeper level of intuition and insight than is usually available during the active periods of daily life. One recovering Catholic I interviewed shared these thoughts on meditation:

> "In 1986 I did a year-long spiritual study course, called 'A Course in Miracles', which at various points teaches meditative skills. I was amazed to experience meditation as a private, intimate relationship with something deeper in me. Lots of people who meditate say that meditation and the feelings that go along with it can't be described in words. While I understand what they mean, I also think this gives meditation an ethereal, surrealistic flavor, and may help keep people away from it, seeing meditation as bizarre, or only for people from California, who will try anything. For me, meditation is a practical as well as a magical experience. It's a way of letting go at the end of the day."

Meditation can offer a sometimes blissful, wonderful high of the type that millions of people are trying to achieve through the use of alcohol or other drugs. The difference is that meditation is not destructive of human creativity or harmful to relationships, but acts to build them up; it does not hurt the body but heals it, and does not promote self-hatred, but encourages self-care.

There are many types of meditation. Some involve the use of a "guide", an inner part of the self who answers questions about important issues in your life. Some meditations require concentration on your breathing, on a mantra, or on a phrase or an idea. Some focus more on emptying, on letting go and waiting to hear or experience what you need to learn about yourself or others. What all forms of meditation share is the assumption that an inner depth of understanding is available to all of us. We need to recognize this in order to let it guide us. We do not need to call this thing God. We can call it "Fred" as long as we recognize it is pretty amazing, and that we are part of it. This understanding, and the process of meditation itself, has nothing to do with religion but can get caught up in religious beliefs for many Catholics who have been taught to trust the Church and its rules and teachings in lieu of listening to their own guidance in spiritual matters. Many of us faithfully followed the teachings until we started coming up against too many obstacles and unanswered questions, and at that point we left the Church. Unfortunately, since the Church was "God" to many of us, we essentially had nowhere to go. The decision to start meditating is a decision to pick up where we left off. A belief in God, per se, is not necessary. "God" is a question of semantics. A recognition of the fact that life is becoming happier and richer is a sign that a loving relationship with yourself and all of creation at a deeper level has begun. To me, the translation of this into daily life is far more important than the language used to describe it. Tuning inward and getting clarity with your deeper self is not an isolating activity, but one that allows a greater sense of compassion and understanding towards everyone you meet in daily life.

BIBLE WORK

We have absorbed and integrated many messages from the Gospels and the Old Testament over the course of our years as Catholics; and while some of these messages may still feel enriching and inspiring to us, others may be limiting, and may create feelings of uncertainty and confusion. As with other work we have done, it is important to recognize the fact that if we haven't consciously worked with a Bible recently (by studying it, questioning it, and considering its meaning), it is likely that the areas of limitation and uncertainty have remained with us and are actively coloring the way in which we live each day, even without our conscious knowledge.

As Catholics, few of us were encouraged to study the Bible. We may have been taught that gospel study led to Luther's pulling away from the Catholic Church and creating his own. The Church for many centuries has instructed its members to seek the advice of clergy when questioning matters of faith. Although an old Boston Catechism depicts a 1950's family sitting and reading the Bible together, few of the questionnaire respondents remember actually reading or studying the Gospels, but only remember hearing them read at Mass on Sunday. Ordinary lay people were not encouraged to question and study the differences between the gospels, which reflect contradictions in story content, flavor, and meaning. That was a job for the priest, Christ's representative. We as lay persons saw ourselves as being many steps removed from God, the Church having convinced us of our need for its exclusive guidance.

Until recently, active exploration of the Bible has been the domain of Church intellectuals: theologians who have debated with one another for centuries over the merits of one text or translation over another. The fact remains that we know very little about Jesus' life, and there is considerable question and uncertainty about what he actually said. Although many Church historians and scholars have knowledge about the New Testament exceeding that of the lay person, each of us is capable of looking at the New Testament as a piece of written material which may have personal meaning for us in some respects, but may feel untrue or irrelevant in others.

This exercise will help to clarify what you already do and do not believe. Go out and buy a Bible (a paperback would be fine). Also buy three highlighters, in different colors. Begin with the New Testament, selecting a chapter or passage to work on. Have your highlighters ready and as you read, highlight in one color the information you do not believe. This could be a quote ostensibly made by Jesus or a description of an event, for example. In another color highlight the passages which have inspired you and which you accept as meaningful or true. With the third, highlight passages which seem confusing or about which you experience conflict. This exercise is not intended as a method of causing divisiveness regarding our beliefs with those of others, but as a means of recognizing that we are unique persons with our own set of convictions, and can be responsible for our own thinking.

Here is an example of how I used this exercise myself, choosing this passage, from Matthew, Chapter 25:

"When the Son of Man comes in his glory, the angels with him, he will sit in state on his throne, with all of the nations gathered before him. He will separate men into two groups, as a shepherd separates the sheep from the goats, and he will place the sheep on his right hand and the goats on his left. Then the king will say to those on his right hand, 'You have my Father's blessing; come, enter and possess the kingdom that has been ready for you since the world was made. For when I was hungry, You gave me food; when, thirsty, you gave me drink; when I was a stranger you took me into your home, when naked you clothed me; when I was ill you came to my help, when in prison you visited me.' Then the righteous will reply 'Lord, when was it that we saw you hungry and fed you, or thirsty and gave you a drink, a stranger and took you home, or naked and clothed you?' And the king will answer, 'I tell you this: anything you did for one of my brothers here, however humble, you did for me'. Then he will say to those on his left hand, 'The curse is upon you; go from my sight to the eternal fire that is ready for the devil and his angels. For when I was hungry you gave me nothing to eat, when thirsty nothing to drink; when I was a stranger you gave me no home, when naked you did not clothe me; when I was ill and in prison you did not come to my help'; and they too will reply, 'Lord, when was it that we saw you hungry or thirsty or a stranger or naked or ill or in prison, and did nothing for you?' And he will answer, 'I tell you this: anything you did not do for one of these, however humble, you did not do for me'. And they will go away to eternal punishment, but the righteous will enter eternal life."

In reading through the text it became clear to me that this work was written by a human being who, like the rest of us, may have been 'divinely' inspired, but who also had a lot of fear. I cannot personally believe that God would think or act like that at the Last Judgment, punishing one group for all eternity and giving eternal life to another. The Church taught me that God had a big tally sheet which kept track of my actions, and that there were black marks made on our souls for every wrongdoing. Our behavior determined whether we would receive fire or glory as punishment or reward. None of this makes any sense to me now, nor does it feel correct intuitively, so I highlighted it in red. On the other hand, the sentence "I tell you this: anything you did for one of my brothers here, however humble, you did for me" seems to speak a message of unity, so I highlighted it in green. I feel I can integrate that message intellectually and feel energized by it, whereas the "fire and glory" message feels negative, scary, and doesn't ring true. I don't believe God would ever want to control me through fear. The whole idea of the Last Judgment as a means for humanity to be unified confuses me right now, so I highlighted it in yellow. This idea feels positive to me but it also seems confusing.

You can move slowly through the New Testament in this manner, thinking and feeling as you go, while identifying what you believe versus what you were taught. In doing this, be prepared for internal resistance. In our family, the Bible was a huge, gold-covered, and ornately decorated book. I would never have vaguely conceived of writing in it. It would have been a sacrilege and a sin; but the adult part of myself has chosen to believe that the Bible was written by ordinary mortals, who were sometimes inspired by deeper parts of themselves but who at other times wrote from the more limited human parts. Because you have both of these elements inside yourself, you can, with practice, begin to hear what feels like truth and what feels like fiction. It doesn't matter that your private truth does not match someone else's. We all have different ways of viewing the world and our own experience, anyway. This process is simply a means of bringing your own understandings into awareness. If the idea of doing this exercise seems too formidable, keep it in the back of your mind as an option for a later stage of the work, do it with the support of a friend, or do it slowly over time.

The Old Testament is a vast, intense, and challenging book. It is seen by the Church as the root source from which Christianity ultimately sprang, and it contains some of the most beautiful, inspiring prose ever written. It also has left many of us with feelings of guilt, fear, sadness and anger, describing a God, *external to the self*, who thunderously rises out of many pages, reminding us repeatedly of what weak and lowly worms we are. The Old Testament to some extent is a mirror of the old fearful thoughts we carry within us, so it too can be a useful tool. Likewise, some passages beautifully reflect love for ourselves and the universe. Going through the Old Testament can be a monumental task, but also highly rewarding as a means of locating the source of our collective guilt and suffering. The Old Testament epitomizes our pain and also our triumph. We now have the option of deciding in which ways we want to maintain its teaching and in which ways we choose to move beyond it. One way of doing this is to adapt Biblical stories in ways that better fit your spiritual views. For example, one recovering Catholic wrote this sardonic, provocative and witty piece, a very different version of the Creation story:

A REVISIONIST ADAM AND EVE

God wanted to celebrate the diversity of creation and so he developed a world that its inhabitants would one day call the Earth. This planet was replete with life of a variety that was a wonder to behold. The most remarkable creature was the human. God had designed this animal from the rich soil of the Earth, and in God's image. Having placed the original individual—who was called Adam—in the Garden, God could see that this prototype needed some work. So, reaching into the region close to Adam's heart, God drew forth the improved version, who was called Eve. God had given

Eve extra genetic material, in the shape of two X chromosomes, unlike the unfortunate Adam, who received one X and a lesser Y chromosome. In Eve's extra DNA was carried the vital information for traits that Adam lacked, such as the ability to communicate or express emotions, and the capacity to find items already in full view without assistance.

With Eve around, Adam's life became more complicated. Unlike Adam, Eve wasn't content to lie around the Garden all day, watching the other animals sport and play. She thirsted after knowledge despite God's dire warnings against trying to attain divine wisdom.

While walking in the Garden one day she came upon the Tree of Wisdom. A large snake (actually Adam's male jealousy of Eve incarnated in phallic form), enticed her into eating of the Tree's fruit. Like Adam, indeed all men past, present and future, the snake was envious of Eve's intelligence, strength, fertility and her ability to find misplaced objects. He urged her to offend God (obviously a male, or how else to explain God's fragile ego?), for then God would cast her out of the Garden and Adam could resume long peaceful days of uninterrupted sport-spectating. The snake hadn't bargained on Eve's persuasive abilities however. When she presented Adam with the fruit, he took a bite.

God, furious at their disobedience, kicked them out of the Garden, condemning them and their offspring to lives of toil and afterlives of Hell. Feeling threatened by Eve's creative abilities, God cursed her, that all humans would be born of pain—their mother's pain.

Adam and Eve went on to raise two sons, Cain and Abel, who later perpetrated the first human tragedy upon each other. They don't call it homicide for nothing. One speculates upon how history would have unfolded had Adam and Eve borne daughters.

What about this insecure, egocentric, and vindictive God? Well, keep in mind that this story was handed down by desert dwellers of the Middle East thousands of years ago. We know about their abiding respect for women. It's wise, when being fed a line, to consider the source.

This woman's characteristic style certainly will not work for everybody, although for her it was obviously engaging and empowering. As always, the emphasis is on finding what *works*, for you. If you find yourself feeling bored, disinterested or turned off at the thought of doing this kind of exercise, stick with it: you may well find that thoughts and feelings will rise to the surface and that the work will engage you in ways you hadn't expected. Take time with this exercise: integrating your beliefs and understandings, on a conscious level, will not happen overnight. Bible work is particularly useful, in that it can help us become aware of the complexity of our own beliefs. For recovering Catholics who may not have opened a Bible in years, it can also help us clarify ways in which are beliefs are still operating in the present.

BIBLIOTHERAPY

Reading can be healing for some of us. This form of healing can be particularly important for recovering Catholics who enjoy study and reading as a matter of course. Some find it helpful to read newer books written by Catholic authors. Newer Catholic literature often contains more hopeful and inspiring messages than those we received in the past. Often, former Catholics are surprised when they hear that changes have occurred in the way in which today's Church views certain formerly intractable issues.

Any reading which emphasizes our inherent worth as human beings can be useful to the process. Many recovering Catholics have explored Eastern writings and traditions, and have been highly enriched by these choices. Organizations such as 'Unity' and 'Science of Mind' have a Christian base but do not hold beliefs related to the concept of sin. 'A Course in Miracles' provides a completely different understanding of Christian principles in a form which many people have found to be empowering. Some recovering Catholics have benefitted greatly by reading Christian authors who are of other denominations. This reading can be particularly appropriate for former Catholics who continue to wish to pursue a Christian way of life, as they may see other denominations as having a "gentler", more eclectic approach: one which puts less emphasis on rules and beliefs, and more on a non-judgmental sharing of experience. Sometimes this focus may result in a decision to become an active member in the religion or spiritual group itself, as in the following:

"All in all, I eventually became pretty unhappy and began to look at other denominations. My husband said he refused to attend the Catholic Church. He wouldn't go because too many of the things the Church stood for were against his beliefs. Eventually, I came across a book that my mother had given me, one of those books that mothers give daughters, and daughters never read. That book (named 'Joshua') helped me to understand that the Church is not what Christ intended, so I kept going in my search. I started attending the Lutheran Church, where I could continue to enjoy some of the rituals that are meaningful to me, like the Apostles Creed, the Nicene Creed, and the Consecration. There was a real spirit of community and people seemed to care and really take time together, not just get in and get out every Sunday. I still call myself a Catholic but go to a wonderful Lutheran Church and my kids are going to be raised Lutheran! That's kind of a hard thought but I know it's a good place to be."

While any general reading can be helpful, honing in on your own specific problem areas is optimal. It is not necessary to center on specifically spiritual or religious texts. Many of the books I have recommended to my clients are oriented towards general mental health. What is important is your awareness *as you read* of the ways in which your Catholic upbringing contributed to those problem areas. As you glance through the list given below, check off any items that represent potential growth areas for you:

1. Sexual enjoyment.
2. Willingness to accept money and other symbols of prosperity.
3. Willingness to put self before others.
4. Willingness to make mistakes as an aid to learning.
5. Openness towards accepting different life views/religious perspectives.
6. Capacity to enjoy pleasure without guilt.
7. Capacity to effectively detach from suffering (low melodrama threshold).
8. Ability to praise oneself freely and abundantly.
9. Ability to make own decisions without guilt.
10. Ability to tolerate ambiguity.

Numerous therapy and self-help books are designed to deal with these and other specific issues that affect many people, including former Catholics. While it is true that non-Catholics also work with some of these issues, the particular intensity of Catholic training (which more than one survey respondent referred to as "brainwashing") cannot be overemphasized. The way we see life's problems and pleasures is in one way or another related to Catholicism, either through the direct teachings of the Church or through the influence of the Catholic *culture*, something which is more obscure and less easily defined. This point is emphasized in the words of one of the survey respondents:

"It's difficult for me to separate the influence of the Church on my life from the effects of growing up Irish. Religion and culture are so tightly interwoven in Irish life that the boundaries blur. My mother never made a loaf of soda bread without blessing it with the shape of a cross in the center before it went into the oven. It made it easier to cut, but was that really the purpose? In countless small ways my life remains marked by this strange legacy. I am constitutionally incapable of letting someone's sneeze go unblessed. My speech is peppered with what we once naively called, with a straight face, ejaculations. I wouldn't be my grandmother's spawn if every third sentence didn't contain a Jesus, Mary or Joseph, or at the least, a Thank God."

Reading with attention paid to the cultural aspects of our Catholic upbringing can enrich the process. In what ways has our lifestyle and family culture changed since leaving the Church? In what ways are these changes beneficial? In what ways do we want to alter family patterns we have developed over time? What traditions and values from our Catholic pasts do we want to incorporate into our lifestyle? It is important to remember that we now have the freedom to order "a la carte". We no longer have to accept all that we were taught, but neither do we have to reject the whole, outright. Provide yourself with the freedom to pick up and put down books at will that fit in with your needs at any given time. As with other healing methods, personal choice and creativity go a long way in working with the process.

CHAPTER ELEVEN

EMBRACING THE GOOD

OR MANY OF US, it is easier and more immediately satisfying to criticize and find fault with our past experience and to blame those whom we see as responsible for these negative experiences as children. While it is useful to get in touch with our feelings of bitterness or hurt as a means of validating them, staying *stuck* in an angry posture and silently holding feelings of resentment only serves to constipate us on an emotional (and perhaps a spiritual) level. It also has the effect of making others responsible for our lives. This may seem to contradict other work we have done, but keep in mind that we are constantly reaffirming the idea of paradox: feeling the feelings *and* letting them go again protects us from falling into the old trap of black and white, dualistic thinking. Acknowledging the mistakes made by the Church and by our parents, as defenders of the faith, while at the same time taking personal responsibility for the choice of whether to hang on to pain and guilt from the past, moves us into an area of

greater complexity, and potentially greater peace of mind.

One way of avoiding the tendency to stay stuck in a blaming mode is to acknowledge the richness of our experience as a Catholics. For some people this can be very difficult, as though the act of acknowledging what "worked" is tantamount to unequivocally embracing the Church again and ignoring its shortcomings. This may feel particularly true to you if your parents or other family members or clergy have "worked" on you to bring you back into the Church. Those who have this experience in mind may have set up a protective barrier to effectively keep the Church—or your families—out. The barrier may accomplish its task, but at the expense of feeling at peace with your decision.

The root of this dilemma seems to come from the Church's teaching of old: you were either *in* the Church or you were *out* of the Church. To be on the fence, so to speak, to have mixed feelings, to be experimenting with your spiritual life: these were not available options. It is essential to reaffirm that it is now okay to have mixed feelings. To heal, we must honor the richness as well as the pain. And paradoxically, some of the old anger and sadness and pain diminishes as we are able to embrace the positive aspects of our earlier life, as expressed by one recovering Catholic:

> "I'm very thankful for the Catholic Church. Some things were very good for me. The *structure* that it offers in a family, for example. I always felt God was there. Take out the guilt and the sin and there were some things I really appreciated. I used the Rosary as a stress management tool. Even now, I can pull out those beads and just the feel of them calms me down and allows me to get sleepy. The Church offered a groundedness: Jesus, Mary, Joseph. They never let you down the way people can."

Often, however, those positive aspects of Catholicism came with a price tag, with stringent conditions attached. The word "but" came into play a great deal here. We could earn our right to heaven *but* we had to be free of sin, *but* we had to fast, *but* we had to wait the prescribed number of hours before receiving Communion. We could be active and play with our friends (other Catholics, of course) *but* we had to be on the lookout for possible occasions of sin. We could get married *but* we had to agree to have children. The list goes on and on. We often lived in a state of anxiety, waiting to fail through sin, and fearing the consequences. We were not unconditionally accepted. We learned that acceptance was based on our behavior, not on the fact that we were alive and wonderful. There were so many rules and conditions and possible hurdles to go through. It is not surprising that as adults we might find it hard to discover the beauty inherent in everyday experience.

Acknowledging possible barriers, then, we need to persist in seeking out the value of our lives as Catholics, not only so that we can honestly evaluate our experience, but also so that we can avoid the polarized thinking that was characteristic of our earlier years. For some of us, this may be an easy process. Past memories, visual images, smells, and delightful emotions may return to you easily and effortlessly. For others it may be like pulling teeth, as you work to let go of the thorns and look at the rose. The positive experiences of one individual can be distressing to another. Memories of incense, statues and holy cards may bring feelings of nostalgia and bliss to one and guilt and anger to another. Likewise, one stage of childhood or adulthood may have been particularly rewarding while another may have been extremely difficult. One respondent felt positive about her Catholic experience as a child, and did not feel anger or pain until her 20's, when she was criticized by her family and by the Church for choosing to marry a non-Catholic. Another struggled through Catholic grade school in misery but later felt delighted reading works by the Catholic theologian Teilhard de Chardin during her college years. And another respondent who lost contact with Catholicism in his teens recalled this childhood experience:

"I loved Confirmation. It was a highlight. It was one of the few events in which I remember feeling high, a real *spiritual* high. It was wonderful. Part of that came from the actual Confirmation, in which I got the name Stanislaus. That was the name I really wanted. The Bishop did those questions and asked me two of them. Out of 200 odd kids that was quite remarkable. There was a special connection between us. Afterwards I remember being told I was a knight (of the Church) and I had an almost out of body experience. Something about the way the words in that ceremony were written was really special. I was reaching the age when you begin to take on responsibility and I felt like I was becoming a man in that ceremony."

Another recovering Catholic viewed rewarding aspects of Catholicism in this way:

"In all fairness, I want to point out that the Church had more than just a negative influence on my life. It's virtually impossible to separate out the cultural influences of a Catholic upbringing. My experience with parochial education is positive—perhaps the nuns were dictatorial and archaic in their methods, but by God we *learned* and I had a far superior education, in my classes of 50-60 kids, sharing books and with no audio-visual equipment, than these more materially blessed kids today will ever receive. They may have beaten it into us, and beaten the spirit out of us, but we *learned.* Not to say that I advocate their methods, but something positive came out of it, and I'll give them that. Also, I've yet to meet a Catholic who was educated by the Church, who didn't have a good grasp of history, world cultures, philosophy and the humanities in general. The Church was such a pervasive power, historically, for so long, that to know the Church is to understand quite a bit about the world. It never ceases to amaze me to realize the bond I have with people who suffered the benefits of a Catholic education. There is a commonality of experience that transcends regional, ethnic, and cultural differences. And for women who were raised Catholic, the shared experiences extend to gender roles and their feelings about womanhood in all aspects of life."

Recalling and reliving positive memories in a quiet, contemplative way can be valuable. When our minds are wound up and we move quickly from one set of past events to another, it can be harder to focus and more difficult to appreciate what enriched and energized us. In quiet, we can more easily get in touch with the positive.

In addition to providing balance for our so-called negative feelings, looking at positive experiences serves another, even more essential purpose: it helps us develop an awareness of our spiritual *base*, the sum total of our unique set of experiences and understandings that have offered the most meaning to us personally. Some of us will return to this spiritual base and discover it is dusty and untouched after years of absence. Many of the survey respondents said they have had no contact with the Catholic Church or with any other Christian churches nor did they have any clarity about what had been valuable in their spiritual experiences as Catholics or in subsequent years, after leaving the Church. These individuals would need support in looking back, as their temptation would be to focus exclusively on all that was wrong. They would need help in looking at what touched them deeply or moved them positively, even without their awareness at the time. The next task would be to remove these experiences from the trappings of Church life and to expand upon them. One question I might ask is: "If barriers and stumbling blocks had not come along to squash your creativity, how might you have developed in a more positive way?" One man told the following story of a moment which felt meaningful to him:

> "In school we were to draw a picture of the Pilgrims giving thanks. I thought the Pilgrims would have been really happy so I drew a picture of them laughing and dancing and frolicking and it felt really good. The nun assumed I had done this to make a mockery of the whole thing and she was enraged. Why would she hate that expression of free joyfulness? It was really ugly to her. She accused me of lots of things: not doing the assignment, trying to screw it up, making a disturbance. I was confused, embarrassed, and felt so bad. I guess I *did* screw this up, I thought. I'm sure I didn't take any liberties with interpretation for a while. It was a cold hand. Whatever impulse I had for being a little zany had cold water poured over it. I've said for years 'I can't draw, I can't sing.' I'm ready to assign my negative judgment on myself to this kind of repression."

In working with him, I asked him to go back in time and, sitting quietly with eyes closed, to see the picture of himself industriously working at his Thanksgiving picture, allowing himself to feel the connection between the Indians and the Pilgrims, to see the dancing, to smell the food cooking, to appreciate the sounds of music and laughing. Because he enjoys writing, I suggested he may want to expand the experience by writing about the scene itself, while allowing himself full freedom to enjoy the connections between the Thanksgiving guests, between himself and the guests, and between himself and the sights, sounds, and smells of the event.

He called me several days later and said that he didn't want to write about it but thought he'd like to do a drawing instead and asked if that would be all right. The first part of the healing process was for me simply to tell him that *of course* it was okay for him to be himself, to do it his own way, allowing his creativity to reveal itself in a way that fit for him. As the second part of this process, I offered him a selection of crayons, markers, and colored pencils and a big piece of paper. I asked him if he could first draw a re-creation of his original Thanksgiving picture, then draw a picture of the scene in the classroom, depicting himself with other students around him, and his teacher standing over him. I then asked him to draw a picture that showed himself and his inner child in a way that would feel helpful, loving, and nurturing. He drew a picture of himself as a little child, showing the adult part of himself looking at the Thanksgiving picture. The adult part is showing interest and warmth and the child is smiling. The colors are very bright and vibrant and the figures are more lifelike than the first picture, and with more detail. He looked pleased with his work. The ways in which the work will affect future creativity remain to be seen. At the moment, it is enough to say that he was able to successfully embrace what was inherently positive in the experience, goodness which up until that time had evaded him due to the fear, anger, and pain which colored his view of the event for all the years that followed the incident.

Embracing the good requires an attitude of creativity and an openness of mind that will allow the inner child to recall with gratitude favorite hymns, prayers, acts of kindness, or whatever else held special meaning for you. The ways in which this is done will reflect your own style and personality. Only *you* know how it felt. You are in the best possible position to create the context for incorporating these memories and experiences into your evolving spirituality or value system.

Another way of working with the good involves clarifying the ways in which your Catholic past has essentially aided in the development of personality traits and characteristics that you treasure in yourself. In reading through the surveys, I identified a set of characteristics that I saw demonstrated over and over in the lives of former Catholics. You can glance through the ones I have named, listed below, or create a list of your own that reflect *your* views. The point is to recognize your present-day successes as intricately woven into that negative life experience.

SOME CHARACTERISTICS OF FORMER CATHOLICS

- Well-read.
- Think independently.
- See themselves as unwilling to lose integrity, or to compromise values or beliefs.
- Tendency to avoid hypocrisy and to dislike manipulation; tendency to express this dislike in direct ways.
- Tendency to distrust organized religion.
- Tendency towards liberal political beliefs.
- Respectful of varied, possibly differing beliefs of others.
- Ability to take a personal stance that may separate them from others but which they see as essential to their well-being.

While many characteristics can vary from individual to individual, based on background, temperament, experience, and personal maturity, those I've mentioned are the ones that are most prominent to *me*. Your own list represents capacities which have in many ways benefitted you. Try to get clear about specifically *how* they have benefitted you. You might also take note of the fact that some of these values were in fact *encouraged* by the Church. One recovering Catholic spoke with great regret when he said: "They gave us this great gift of thinking... and then encouraged us to turn it all off." The Church may have essentially rejected some of your values, but it is no longer necessary to deny them yourself.

Embracing the good is especially necessary for recovering Catholics who say, when asked to do these exercises, "Can't think of much". These individuals are often in touch with the anger they feel regarding their family of origin, or clearly remember the horrors they have endured at school. However, it is important not to throw the baby out with the bathwater: there are always positive aspects of experience intermingled with the negative. Some of the clients I have worked with have been able to achieve this by closing their eyes, getting into a relaxed, composed state, and allowing their minds to recall bits and pieces of information that feel hopeful and happy, while intentionally "kicking out" pieces of information that feel fearful, hurtful, or limiting. It's not that this information is not important—it simply belongs in another exercise. If ideas are not forthcoming, let go, while expressing an internal willingness to let information float to the surface. This may come in the form of dreams, while daydreaming, or through associations in your everyday life. One woman described her experience with this exercise:

> "I really started off having trouble with this. I just couldn't think of anything that felt really good about those years. I *do* think I block out the good experiences as a type of protection for myself, though. I'm still worried after 25 years that the Church is going to pull me back in if I don't keep a watchdog at the gate. In fairness to them, I'm willing to acknowledge that this is of my own doing. When I started to think about doing the exercise I found that I suddenly needed to make a pot of coffee. Then I remembered that I couldn't drink coffee with my eyes closed. Then I had to go

to the bathroom, then the phone rang and of course I had to answer it. All in all, about three hours went by before I sat down to do it. I was able to see what I was doing. I'm still mad at the Church and I just didn't want to give them any satisfaction by remembering good stuff. I also eventually realized that this didn't make sense because I was doing the exercise for *myself*. Finally, I sat down and was able to get into a quiet frame of mind. At that point, some nice things related to my aunt, who was a nun, came to mind, as did a few other things connected with Christmas—with midnight Mass, which has a lot of good memories connected with it. In looking back, I think it was necessary for me to go through all of that resistance, or advance preparation, so that I could feel safe and clear with myself that thinking positive things is not a recommitment to the Church."

Embracing the good is a way of valuing the richness of your own personality. All of the things you appreciate in yourself arose within the context of your family life as a Catholic, and in your school and Church life. Allow your awareness to develop as time moves on, acknowledging the best of the past by seeing it as rich soil, prepared carefully by you, with the primary intention of bringing forth new growth.

FORGIVENESS

Forgiveness is a word that may carry with it reminders of sugar-coated sermons, lectures, and texts which urged us to "turn the other cheek" and show brotherly love in our contacts with others. The great shining example of forgiveness was Jesus himself, who asked at the time of the Crucifixion that God forgive those who were harming him, since they did not know what they were doing. If Jesus was able to recommend forgiveness under these circumstances, it was our duty to forgive others who might offend us in far less serious ways. We learned that we were more saintly if we could simply ignore the behavior of the other guy. It was, in fact, this act of ignoring the behavior of the person who offended us that made our act of forgiveness so noble. We were taught to rise above the situation and say "he doesn't know what he's doing". The problem, however, was that most of us were not saints and often harbored resentful feelings about the behavior of that other person. We *said* we had forgiven, while secretly we held onto our anger, and our feelings of pain, fear and guilt. This applied not only to daily life events, among our friends and family, but it also carried into our relationship with God. As little children we tended to project our assumptions about ourselves onto God. If *in our hearts* we weren't able to truly forgive other people for their actions, we assumed that God wouldn't forgive us for *our* indiscretions, either! I believe it is for this reason that many former Catholics report having gone to Confession weekly without ever feeling truly forgiven. The clergy, acting as representatives of God, often confirmed that we were right in our view: we *would* never be good enough. This was also underlined, as we have seen, by teachings surrounding Original Sin. As a result of all these negative associations, it is not surprising that recovering Catholics often cringe when I recommend that they do some forgiveness work. The method I want to suggest, however, is quite different from that of our childhood.

Forgiveness incorporates two distinct, but complementary processes:

1) The "offense" in question is named and acknowledged, and the resulting feelings are carefully identified. In Chapter 7 Jeff became clear that he had felt wronged by Sister R., and he identified his feelings of anger and humiliation. Jeff did not "turn the other cheek" in the sense of letting the whole issue go (he had in fact attempted to do that for years without suc-

cess); instead, he recognized that her behavior was not okay and was no more okay today than it was in 1963.

2) The person offended expresses a willingness (to himself and ideally to another person acting as a witness) to relinquish those feelings that have plagued *him* for all of these days, months, or years. True forgiveness signifies an internal desire to free *the self*, which generally causes the whole event to assume lesser significance. This doesn't happen by turning the other cheek, but is simply a natural consequence of releasing the feelings. Again, this does *not* imply that the offending person is being relieved of their accountability for their behavior.

As former Catholics we may find we have a long list of individual people with whom we remain emotionally entangled. Take time to compile this list, carefully. In some cases you may feel that an offense was definitely committed by another person. At other times, you may be unsure as to who was in the "wrong" and who was in the "right". Or you may be clear that *you* intentionally or unintentionally hurt another person. Take the time to sort out the feelings that arise, and in each case work to let the feelings go, through journalling, mirror work, visualization, letter-writing, dance, art, or any number of other ways that may occur to you. Again, there is no correct way to do this work. It is useful, however, to make sure that your own feelings are being expressed initially before you move on to the releasing stage, so as to avoid the tendency to forgive on the more superficial basis we were accustomed to in childhood. In doing his Thanksgiving Day pictures referred to earlier, my client could have moved on to doing forgiveness work with the sister who had been unkind to him, by drawing a picture of himself expressing his feelings of anger and humiliation to her directly, and then, by drawing a picture of himself doing a dance while letting these same feelings go. He could also have done a picture of himself resolving the issue with the sister.

One client who enjoys dancing made up a three part dance while doing forgiveness work related to a priest who had touched her sexually during grade school days. In the first section she played the part of the priest, whom she saw as an ominous, frightening person. She decided not to enact the abuse itself, but allowed the dance to express the fearful nature of the situation. In the second section she played herself, expressing a combination of shame, fear, and pleasure at receiving attention from this man, whom she had previously idolized. In the third section she enacted her feelings flowing away from her as she expressed increased feelings of power and control over her own body.

Dance may not be right for you. The point is to think about what kind of expression *could* work. One client who is a construction worker would line up boards to be cut and imagined that each one represented his feelings of shame related to being beaten by his father for the sin of masturbation. He then went back and cut the boards, mentally signifying his willingness to let go of the shame and the accompanying anger.

Keep in mind that this work doesn't have to be done in a day, or in some perfect way. There are no rules to govern your decisions about how to proceed. Give yourself a wide berth, and trust your intuition.

CHAPTER TWELVE

LAST WORDS

I HAVE PURPOSEFULLY avoided focusing on the option of returning to the Church as a means of working through old issues; and I have avoided this out of a belief that the majority of recovering Catholics are no longer interested in returning to Catholicism as a way of life. In spite of this, a return to Catholicism is nevertheless an option as a way of healing. I do consider it possible to be both a recovering and a practising Catholic today, as evidenced by some of the clients I have worked with; although I sense that this will continue to be somewhat uncommon. A number of former Catholics have responded to the Church's attempts to reach out to them through the Renew program, which offers its member a forum in which to express their feelings of anger, resentment, pain, and fear. The Renew program also acts to clarify issues of faith, and to provide former Catholics with an update of changes in the Church. For some former Catholics this program can beneficial. It can provide a great opportunity to talk about the pain connected with Catholicism, with a present-day Catholic priest, nun or lay person who is willing to listen empathically to that pain, to acknowledge its effect in your life, and essentially to apologize on behalf of the Church. Some people go to the Renew program simply to release their pent-up feelings, without wanting to re-connect with the Church in any way. Some go to see if the Church has changed sufficiently in specific areas. One Catholic woman, who had been denied supportive help from the Church when she opted for a divorce in the 1960's, returned to the Church in the 1970's and had this to say about her experience:

> "I left the Church for about 10 years after my divorce while in my mid 40's. I felt totally alone. I saw discrimination against women very plainly. I still see that today, but things are chang-ing. I didn't attend other churches but I have watched the Church accept all Christians equally and other religions at least with respect. It makes me very happy because it's finally what I can really believe. I'm still arguing women's rights but they'll come—everything else has. When I came back (to the Church) it was totally different—it was amazing."

This woman decided to go back to the Church itself for heal-ing, and felt that sufficient change had occurred for her to want to reconnect. She joined a parish that she saw as progressive and supportive, and this aided the healing process.

Many present day Catholics no longer see themselves exclu-sively as members of a larger body which interprets God's desires and plans for them; instead, they consider that God is *within* them, a concept which can have the result of giving them much greater autonomy and the ability to make their own decisions about issues such as birth control, abortion, and homosexuality (as well as lesser issues, such as the need for weekly Mass atten-dance). In previous decades the decisions made by clergy were accepted unconditionally. These days, this is often not the case: in fact, some matters of faith are even questioned by the clergy who represent the Vatican.

While returning to the Church may be an option for some, it is not for others, for a variety of reasons. Survey respondents were asked if they could see themselves returning to the Church under certain circumstances. They were also asked to talk about spiritual practices and/or beliefs which have acted as personal anchors since leaving the Church. Here is a sample of responses.

"Emphatic 'no'—I would not return. I cannot be part of a corrupt system. I disagree with the hierarchy, the administration, the Pope, and most of the teachings of the Church. I think it is very narrow and limiting and very chauvinistic."

"During high school religion classes I heard that I should stop asking questions. 'This is the teaching of the Church, take it or leave it.' So I left it. I have studied numerous religions in the course of schooling and in outside reading. I believe they have provided a good rudimentary view of how religion functions in society to give the individual a fixed view of the world and provide for social adhesion and help to give an answer to some of life's mysteries. I wouldn't go back to Catholicism because, in light of the above, I'm no longer strictly Christian in the philosophical department."

"No. There are too many differences I have with the Church, most of which are political. I have not formalized my feelings at this point though I'm not ready to give up completely. There are probably more positives within the Catholic Church than most organized religions (as far as my own personal style goes) and there are many good people working within the Church, but too many things would need to change for me to want to go back."

"I still call myself a Catholic (by culture) but do not go to Church. The Church is too rigid and judgmental and patriarchal. If the Church became more open and less judgmental I might consider going back. I fight for justice and equality in my work (social work) every day—I need a religious community where I don't feel I have to fight for openness and non-judgmental attitudes.

Right now I'm looking at other non-Catholic churches but this is difficult because I was raised so Catholic that leaving the Church has created feelings of guilt as though I had been brainwashed."

"No. I now regard the Catholic Church as a personal disaster for me, a totally regrettable experience. On the other hand I see that it has done a lot of good for people, mostly in consoling them about the wretchedness of life on earth. Intellectually it remains for me the grossest of absurdities. The new insight is that an institution can have the metaphysics all wrong and still be a good help to many people. Personally, I would never go back. I can't imagine such a change. A religion that was acceptable to me—earth-centered, mystical, respectful of life, egalitarian—would bear no resemblance to the Catholic Church."

"No. Many things didn't make sense or seemed hypocritical. Since leaving I've dabbled in acting, which provides a forum for some soul-searching and learning. I wouldn't return to the Church. The changes would have to be so broad that it wouldn't in any way resemble the Catholic Church".

"I'm not a Catholic now. I believe it has changed a lot in rites and rituals since I left, with less rigidity, etc., but the Infallibility of the Pope will always be its downfall. I have attended the Episcopal Church, Unity, and done Transcendental Meditation. I now follow the teachings of the Path of Masters. It's a path that teaches the realization of God through meditation and instruction by a Living Master—a Path of *Love*."

"No. For me the hypocrisy within the Church seems perennial, and I can't buy it. The Church taught us one set of standards and did another as far as I'm concerned. The Church said to love the poor, while it went about amassing riches, to love one another while it hurt little kids if they goofed up in class, to love one another, but do as I say. Lately I've become aware that the 'new' Church, which is supposed to be so much more accepting, really consists of only a *group* of people within the Church. This new group seems to encourage people to do what they want to do, even though that may be way out of the ball park in terms of what the Church teaches or what the priest in that parish thinks. Recently I looked back into the Church and that's what I found. To me, it just felt like more hypocrisy. It also seemed like there was a lot of confusion and disagreement. I feel like the Church's influence was hurtful in my childhood. I don't want to spend half of my adulthood not only dealing with my own issues, but the Pope's too! I do have a spiritual life, just based on connecting up with other people warmly whenever I can."

"No, nor Christian—I am agnostic; I neither believe, nor disbelieve in 'God' (because it partly depends on the definition) and don't consider the question especially important. The Catholic Church is still a community potentially valuable to its members (though not one I can join, since I don't share their beliefs). In general, I feel all religions are fatally flawed, even though they may have much good. I left when

I was 18—in the midst of a theological discussion with my Mom, when I realized that I was speaking of *other people's concepts* of my experience, rather than my own; I decided then to take St. Paul's advice and to speak only what I have seen with my own eyes. I said my last prayer—asking for proof, if there was any, and promising to heed it if shown—and then proceeded to limit my beliefs to my own experience, and my faith to that indicated by my own experience. Since then I have generally been at a much greater spiritual peace than before."

"No. If I was asked to talk to the Church about my views, I'd say 'Get with the program!' They have made some favorable changes and some parishes are keeping pace with reality. They foster a nice sense of 'community' and helping others, but the beliefs are still too conservative for me. I *do* like the idea of my kids going to a Church, but Catholicism is too conservative, with their views on birth control, homosexuality, and abortion. I'm not Christian though I have taught my children some Christian views; but I present these in the light of '*some* people believe Christ was God, some don't.' Variety in beliefs and customs is great and shouldn't be a problem! We're all searching to understand God."

Another reason some people have for remaining outside the Church is related to the issues of humor and humility within the Church hierarchy. It is helpful to look into the background and continued practices of the hierarchy so as to provide an understanding of this decision. We were part of the "One, Holy, Catholic and Apostolic Church", and there was nothing funny about that. The Church carried with it an atmosphere of seriousness. The Church represented Christ on earth. As such, it had a mission: to teach Christ's message, a message of love tempered with justice (leftover from the Old Testament). In one interviewee's words:

"Nowhere in the Gospels do we hear of Christ goofing around, telling jokes, and laughing either at himself or at the incongruities he experienced. *That* would have been useful reading!"

His attendance at the wedding feast at Canna doesn't give an understanding of the lighter side of Jesus' life, although it is used often by Christian churches as an indicator that Jesus was "just like us".

So much of what we heard about Jesus centered on the Crucifixion and on the need for dealing with our guilt—all serious stuff. Laughing in Church was verboten for both adults and children alike. Again, the idea of dualism comes into play. It's almost as though the Church believed that breathing lightness into Jesus' life or the life of the Church would result in destruction of the faith. Although some former Catholics may be surprised to hear that people these days do laugh in a Catholic Church, this has certainly been a new development and one that very much reflects the personality of the clergy in an individual parish. Most of those interviewed felt that the superficial changes with reference to the atmosphere (for example better music, lay involvement) could not alter the Church hierarchy's perceived need for continued control over the lives of Church members.

Thinking about and questioning the faith, its traditions and its beliefs was not encouraged by the Church itself as I was growing up, and despite the advent of guitar Masses and ecumenical services, this continues to be discouraged by the Church, in both small and larger ways. An example of the latter is the recent de-frocking of Matthew Fox, a liberated and free-thinking Dominican priest. Some may disagree with his writings but what is most unfortunate is the fact that the Church hierarchy chose to see them as heresy.

This is the same as a child in a family being denied the right to his own opinion. Both the child and his family suffer.

The Church hierarchy used a heavy hand to keep its members in check over the course of the 20th century. Church tradition is steeped in an atmosphere of loyalty to the past: loyalty to previous traditions instituted by various popes in various time periods, and loyalty to the *illusion* that these men were supermen. While leaders of *countries* are able and certainly willing to look at the roles their predecessors played in influencing present-day events, Popes, who seem to see themselves as different, more capable, or more enlightened than their lay counterparts, act as though the decisions of previous generations of Popes are indistinct from their own, and this helps to maintain the impression of uniformity and order. The difficulty is, however, that many of us are now aware that change is the mainstay of life, and we believe that confusion, uncertainty, clarity, and resolution are all a part of daily life. Many former Catholics have stated they will not accept spiritual direction without an acknowledgment of the fallibility of its leaders. When has a Pope discussed his own decisions, while candidly reviewing the successes and difficulties of his predecessor? The ultimate irony, of course, is that many members of the Church have been lost over the past 20 years for these very reasons. The Church seems to lack an element vital to its own survival: the capacity to look, *with humility* at its own pronouncements, values, and edicts, particularly when they become *obscure* or *outdated.* While many of the laity are able to laugh at situations, events, and memories that are funny in their Catholic pasts, and while clergy no doubt do the same, in private, the clergy in today's Church must publicly sit on the fence, in many situations, showing respect for the Church's hierarchy and traditions while acknowledging the needs of many of its parishioners for increased freedom of expression.

This seems to result in what one respondent called the "yes-but" syndrome. She went back to the Church after a period of absence to see how Catholicism had changed. She attended a group designed to welcome back former Catholics to the Church. She was pleased to feel welcomed, and pleased that the Church accepted her. She was aware of a focus on community and positive social and interdenominational contacts. In time, she also became aware that certain elements necessary to her spiritual growth were missing, namely, the ingredient of humor at the Church's own foibles, and a spirit of humility in the way the Church regarded itself. Her particular way of moving forward in the face of this was to attend both Catholic and other denominational churches concurrently. She continues to respect and love aspects of the Church and its traditions, but is not waiting for it to make changes necessary for her own spiritual survival.

Humor and Catholicism don't mix. Humility and Catholicism don't mix. This is not to say that lay persons were not encouraged to seek humility. We were. It is not to say that good jokes haven't been told, by clergy and lay people alike. They were. The issue is more related to the Church and its ability to laugh at its own foibles and shortcomings, as I've said. What would need to happen for the Church to speak openly about its financial assets, its shortage of priests, its difficulty in meeting the needs of its members in a complicated age? This is clearly a different kind of position, and one that would require honest self-appraisal. It would involve the Church doing what Alcoholics Anonymous calls a 'First Step', by admitting that it is experiencing powerlessness. It would involve the Church's hierarchy coming out from behind the shield of Infallibility in order to deal with its members on a flesh-and-blood level, and admitting that, in many issues, the Vatican is floundering just like the rest of us. Can you imagine the Pope and the Cardinals admitting they feel powerless and that the Church is not working in some respects? Can you imagine them admitting that it has been and is dysfunctional in some ways? That it needs help, reorganization, new blood, and changes in structure, particularly of a financial and political nature? That harm has been done in its name to individuals and groups? Perhaps all of this *will* occur in centuries to come.

I would like to conclude with a favorite quote from one recovering Catholic. I enjoyed the freedom of expression, the humor, and the creativity inherent in his words:

> "The Church has changed, yes. People touch the Eucharist. The service has changed; but a lot of it seems superficial to me. It doesn't effect the deeper issues because of the profound contradictions that I just don't believe will ever change, mainly, the issue of the 'One, True Church'. It's such a great way to keep the party faithful. Why would they change that? It all comes back to the idea of openness of thought. You would always come to a point in discussing things with a priest who says he is open-minded about spirituality and at that point the party line comes in and you can go no further.

> "What would need to change for me to want to be a member of the Church again? Drop the Infallibility of the Pope. Drop the idea of Jesus as the only Son of God. It's hard to answer because you'd have to go back and start at the beginning! Start with the idea of God coming down into Christ's body. Big deal! God came down in everybody's body! That's my belief now, so it would make the Church unrecognizable."

Clearly, there are many recovering Catholics for whom a return to the Church is not a viable option. Some of us no longer feel the need to work out our conflicts *within* the Church, and are comfortable having made the decision to move on in life and explore other options. This needs to be acknowledged as a legitimate option; at the same time we must recognize that our Catholic roots can never be truly severed; as John put it, we've got "Catholic molecules," and why would we want these roots to be severed? Some of our greatest strengths have developed as a direct result of our Catholic pasts. We can stay stuck in our resentments and pain; we can remain in a state of denial, trivializing and discounting the impact of the past; or we can choose to use that experience as a background from which to paint new pictures of what we truly want in our present-day lives.